Oregon's Fading Past

Lawrence E. Nielsen
Donald S. Galbreath

Co-Researcher
Deanne M. Nielsen

Editors
Beverly H. de Young
Linda N. Hickel
Barbara Murry

— A Maverick Publication —

ISBN 0-89288-240-9

Library of Congress Catalog Card Number: 93-78973

Maverick Publications, Inc.
P.O. Box 5007
Bend, Oregon 97708

Table of Contents

Preface

This book is about many of the pioneers who settled east of the Cascade Mountains in Oregon. In writing this book, the authors were faced with the difficult task of selecting pioneers to include in the book. They used the following selection criteria to determine the candidates:

- Only those pioneers whose graves have been located and visited by the authors were selected.

- Pioneers selected were usually the first settlers in an area or county.

- People who were influential or notorious have been included.

- Any person born before 1800, with a known gravesite, has been included.

- Veterans of the Civil War were given special consideration.

- Pioneers who experienced unique or spectacular events were selected as they are of interest to most readers.

The authors made their selection on the basis of the above criteria and on their personal interests. Undoubtedly, another researcher would have chosen different candidates for the list, but the authors are confident that the majority of the pioneers chosen would appear on both lists. The authors' list includes over 550 pioneers.

The authors read thousands of pages of history to determine who were the earliest and most important pioneers. The authors found the most useful sources to be county histories published at the turn of the century and those published in the 1980's. These history books give biographical information about the pioneers. After compiling the list of candidates, the authors then visited cemeteries in order to locate individual tombstones.

The authors have included specific examples of *Oregon's Fading Past* in the second section of the book. These examples include disintegrating pioneer buildings, ghost towns and remnants of pioneer roads. Swiftly these buildings are disappearing, as have their inhabitants. This book is the authors' attempt to preserve, through documentation, a portion of this valuable pioneer heritage.

This book could not have been written without the help of Deanne Nielsen, our co-researcher. When author Lawrence Nielsen became too ill to continue the field work of visiting cemeteries, Deanne and Don Galbreath finished the field work. Still, this work is not actually complete, as some pioneers in several counties remain undocumented.

The authors are especially grateful for the extensive biographical information supplied by three women—Sherry Kaseberg of Sherman County, Anita Drake of Wasco County, and Irene Helms of Crook County. They supplied much of the biographical data for these three counties.

Many people have contributed information used in this book. The authors wish to acknowledge and thank the following people:

Marguerite Allman, Irving & Linda Anderson, Lewis J. Ansell, Mary Bales, Grace Bartlett, Diane Berry, Allen Bidiman, Julia (Sutherland) Bowdle, Bob Busakke, Dan Carver, Gene & Ruth Cholin, Keith & Donna Clark, Reg Cole, Don Cowdrey, Raymond Crum, Ms. Jerry De Priest, Beverly de Young, Bill & Joe Dressel, Jack Evans, George Fax, Luella Friend, Mrs. Bun Gilchrist, Mike Hanley, Joseph Irby IV, Jim Johnson, Nyna Knighten, Maureen (Mrs. Clint) Krebs, Mrs. Beatrice Lavadour, LDS Genealogical Library, Donald Leigh, Bob Lovgren, Ralph Marlatt, Tom McDonald, Jim Melvin, Barbara Murry, Elmer Newton, Frank & Maggie Nielsen, Mary Noble, Joe O'Connor, Mary Oman, Bill Phillips, Tom Rachau, Virginia Roberts, Francis Juris Rush, Chet & Kathleen Schott, Donna Still, Jean Shaw, Pete Srack, Cora Stubblefield, Jack Sturtevant, George Sutherland, Pearle Sutherland, Ardyce Swift & Redmond Library Staff, Daryl Swyer, Patrick Thompson, Alma Jean Tipley, Faye Waheneka, Don Watson.

Part 1

SEARCHING FOR TOMBSTONES

What type of people would study tombstones?
History buffs, who are curiosity prone.
They're willing to crawl through the briers and brambles,
Where strange creepers crawl and snakes like to ramble.
They also research the well groomed plots,
Where beauty brings serenity to their thoughts.
For best results, all must work as a team,
Areas are assigned, and each has a scheme.
In the authors situation, it's a family affair
Where each personality shows its own flair.
Deanne leads the pack as she's a quick spotter,
Larry's heavy equipment makes him a slow plodder.
Barb takes to the hilltops for she likes fresh air,
Maggie looks for inscriptions, like "killed by a bear."
Bev reads so many markers her mind goes blank,
Was she looking for Henry, Homer or Hank?
Frank moves with quiet reverence and anticipation,
While Don, in far corner, analyzes the situation.
Beth listens intently to the stories we perceive
From facts that were gathered and tales they must weave.
So, if you are interested in solving a mystery,
Buried in a cemetery is much interesting history.

Written by
Beverly Nielsen de Young

Chapter 1

Introduction

As the author, Lawrence Nielsen, worked his way through thousands of pages of eastern Oregon county histories published at the turn of the century and in the 1980's, he discovered an immensely diverse assortment of pioneer biographies. He was excited to find that the grand nephew of a signer of the Declaration of Independence is buried near Prineville, while Redmond is the burial site of a royal princess who was related to Queen Victoria. Linus Pauling, the winner of two Nobel Prizes, has a grandfather buried in the Condon Cemetery. One of Oregon's most famous authors, Frederick Homer Balch, who wrote *The Bridge of the Gods*, rests in the Lyle, Washington Cemetery. A survivor of the Whitman Massacre is buried in the Haystack Cemetery near Spray.

These are just a few of the several hundred pioneers who settled Eastern Oregon that are discussed in this book. They include miners, ranchers, merchants, politicians, and professional people. Men are generally given the most publicity in the settlement of frontier regions. However, their wives and other women should be given equal credit. These women worked beside their husbands, raised large families, often taught their children, and brought culture to the new communities. Many wives died at an early age during childbirth. Other wives had to bear the sorrow of the death of many of their children over a short period of time from such diseases as diphtheria.

Many tens of thousands of pioneers came to Oregon between 1843 and 1880. Most of these people moved to the western part of the state. Nevertheless, there were thousands of people who became the original settlers of Oregon east of the Cascade Mountains. Most of these people led quiet lives that drew little attention. Some of these early settlers, however, became very prominent and important citizens for a variety of reasons.

If you were to ask the average person who the earliest and most important pioneers were in their area, most people would find it difficult to name even a few of these pioneers, let alone tell you where they are buried. We are going to give a short biography of many of these important pioneers along with their burial location. With thousands of possible candidates to choose from, we had to drastically limit the number that could be included in this book. The pioneers selected had to be important for some particular reason. For example, they may have been the first settlers of an area, or they may have held some important political office. Some dramatic incident may have occurred in their life, or they may have become prominent business people or ranchers. Finally, the authors' most important selection criterion was that the candidate's burial site be located and their tombstone be viewed by the authors or by their co-researchers before they were included in this book.

Undoubtedly, some of the most important early pioneers have been excluded from our list. The authors may not have been aware of their important contributions, or not sufficient biographical information could be found on them. In many cases, we were unable to find their tombstone.

The pioneers who ventured to Oregon often showed two characteristics. First, they were restless people. They might have made half a dozen to a dozen major moves during their lifetimes. They may have started from Europe or the East Coast and moved several times before reaching the Mississippi or Missouri Rivers. Many participated in the California Gold Rush before arriving in Oregon. Others took the Oregon Trail to the Willamette Valley. From the Willamette Valley, they moved back to the area east of the Cascade Mountains in order to mine for gold, raise cattle or sheep, farm, or start a business. A large number of pioneers crossed the United States at least three times. They went from Oregon or California to their old homes in the East to bring their families West or to marry sweethearts and bring their new wives to Oregon.

This restless tendency often makes it difficult to locate their graves. After living in a place for many years and having made a name for themselves there, they suddenly moved to an entirely different area. For example, the founder of Waterman is buried in The Dalles. Gales Creek near Forest Grove is named for Joseph Gale, a very prominent citizen of that area. He is buried in Richland in Northeastern Oregon.

A second characteristic of most of the pioneers was that they were jacks-of-all-trades. During his lifetime, a pioneer might be a miner, a blacksmith, a stage coach driver, a merchant, and a rancher. A sheepherder might become a doctor by studying books while he was herding the sheep!

The authors visited several hundred cemeteries during the years required to research this book. Some of these cemeteries, especially the larger ones, are maintained. However, many of the cemeteries are in a disgraceful state of neglect. This is especially true of many of the earliest, small cemeteries where pioneers are buried. These cemeteries are overgrown with grass, weeds, and brush. Many tombstones are broken or have tumbled down. Tombstones lying in grass and weeds deteriorate much more rapidly than the upright stones. Decaying vegetation produces acids which rapidly disintegrate the stones and make the inscriptions difficult to read. The authors strongly suggest that community volunteer groups make a project of cleaning up, repairing, and protecting these neglected cemeteries. Church groups, Boy Scouts, or business organizations could take the initiative to restore and preserve these cemeteries, which are such an important part of our heritage.

A number of cemeteries have suffered from vandalism. Thoughtless, inconsiderate people have toppled many of the tombstones in some cemeteries. Distressing examples include the Harney Cemetery east of Burns and the Pioneer Cemetery in Huntington. Teenagers removed the tombstones from the Huntington Cemetery and left them in the road. They were forced to return the stones to the cemetery, but an old-timer told the authors that the tombstones were not returned to their proper places! To make matters worse, there often is not enough local pride to restore the tombstones back to their original condition. At the Kees Cemetery near Weston, vandals not only toppled most of the tombstones but then broke them into many pieces with sledge hammers! The Foster Cemetery near Stanfield and the old Milton-Freewater Cemetery near the water tower are in a disgraceful state of disrepair and neglect and are completely covered with sagebrush.

The location of the burial places of many of our pioneers have been permanently lost. Since tombstones were difficult to obtain for isolated areas, pioneer graves were often marked by a board or wooden cross. These markers rapidly decayed and disappeared. Unless a pioneer had children or good friends who later installed a tombstone, the sites of the grave became impossible to locate. In the bustling activity of mining camps, there were many men who were unknown to their companions. Many such early pioneers are in graves with simple tombstones designated only as "Unknown." In some cases, the inscriptions on tombstones were not deeply chiseled into the stone. After a hundred years or so, the inscriptions on such stones are no longer legible.

In old cemeteries, there is a great variety of tombstones. There are upright slabs, tall monuments, obelisks, and giant blocks on which are inscribed the name, dates of birth and death, and other information about the person buried there. Contrast these stones with the drab slabs at ground level or below found in most modern cemeteries, and one can certainly see the appeal of the old-style tombstones!

As we viewed thousands of tombstones, it was interesting to note how popular names have changed over the years. A hundred and fifty years ago, popular names for women included Lucinda, Lavina, Carrie, Melvina, Sarah, Maria, Amanda, Martha, Susan, Phoebe, Lodema, Sophia, Hattie, Minerva, Mattie, Rebecca, Almira, and Pamelia. Popular names for men included Luther, Jeremiah, Joshua, Eli, Francis, Ezekial, Isaac, Horace, Jacob, Peter, Perry, Elijah, Jesse, Enoch, and Hiram. Other names seem to be favorites forever. For women, these names include Mary, Elizabeth, Nancy, Jane, and Margaret. For men, these names include Robert, William, James, Joseph, Thomas, and John.

The authors have attempted to keep errors in this book to a minimum, but certainly some errors do exist. This book contains thousands of dates and hundreds of names of pioneers. Often dates and spelling of names on tombstones do not agree with historical reference works. In addition, some reference works are known to be inaccurate in many cases. As a result, errors result when these references are used. At times, the authors have included two dates or two different spellings when there is doubt.

Various parts of Eastern Oregon were settled at different times. Wasco County had its first pioneers in the 1850's and 60's. The gold-mining Baker and Grant Counties rapidly became populated in the 1860's. Cattle and sheep ranchers became the pioneers of Sherman and Gilliam Counties in the 1870's and 1880's. Wallowa County received its first pioneers in the 1870's. Much of Deschutes and Jefferson Counties were not settled until after 1900 when irrigation projects made farming practical and improved transportation made the lumber industry profitable.

Disintegrating tombstones and unkept cemeteries are not the only examples of our fading past. Pioneer buildings are rotting away, being torn down, or burned. Each year, more of these buildings disappear forever. Remnants of pioneer roads are rapidly disappearing too. These roads gradually disappear by natural processes or, in many cases, are destroyed by new road construction, plowed up to make more land for farming, or are destroyed by housing developments.

The second part of this book illustrates some of these examples of *Oregon's Fading Past*. Examples include disintegrating homestead cabins, barns, old churches, ghost town's businesses and schools, stage stations, and remnants of pioneer roads. Photographs are used to document the remnants of our pioneer heritage. These pioneer buildings and roads create an outdoor museum which provide current visitors with a trip back into *Oregon's Fading Past* and an appreciation for Oregon's pioneer history.

In the biographical sketches, the pioneer's name is introduced by using capital letters if his or her tombstone was found. Other pioneers who might be mentioned are not in capital letters.

The Earliest Pioneers

We should remember that the Indians were the first pioneers to the Oregon Territory thousands of years before the appearance of the white man. Most Indians did an amazing amount of traveling during the course of a year. They might travel to the Columbia River or another river for salmon. They might journey to the mountains to hunt deer. And, they would go to such places as Big Summit Prairie or Camas Prairie to get camas, a major source of food for many tribes. Over the years, trails developed which followed the easiest and most practical routes from one place to another. As a result of their extensive travels, the Indians acquired an intimate knowledge of large territories.

The first white men to visit Oregon were the fur trappers and explorers. They followed the Indian trails, and generally employed Indians as guides. In later years, nearly all the pioneer wagon roads followed the Indian trails as closely as possible. Thus, the Indians greatly facilitated the settling of Oregon by the white man.

Trappers and mountain men often took Indian wives and lived with the Indians. Some of their children became prominent in pioneer days.

The Indians were generally peaceful people towards the white settlers. A number of individual Indians stand out in their assistance to the early settlers. We shall mention one example.

JEAN BAPTISTE CHARBONNEAU was the son of Sacajawea, the famous Indian guide and interpreter for the Lewis and Clark Expedition. He was born February 11, 1805 in a Mandan village in North Dakota. His father was a French Canadian, Toussaint Charbonneau. Although Jean might not be considered an Oregon pioneer, he spent much of his first and second years in Oregon, and he died in southeast Oregon. Captain William Clark adopted Jean and gave him a good education. He lived in

Germany for six years travelling with a German prince. Jean spoke English, German, French, Spanish, and Indian. He trapped for the American Fur Company for fifteen years. He was in California during the Mexican War as a guide for the military. He mined gold in California and then left for the gold mines in Montana. At Inskeep's (Inskip's) Station in southeastern Oregon west of Jordan Valley, he contracted pneumonia and died May 16, 1866. He is buried with others at the Inskeep Station by the ghost town of Danner.

Chapter 2
Pioneers Born Before 1800

There are very few pioneers buried in eastern Oregon who were born before 1800. Even if a pioneer came to Oregon with the first parties to use the Oregon Trail when it originated in 1843, the emigrant went to the Willamette Valley. Therefore, the pioneer had to be at least 43 years old when he or she arrived in Oregon. It was years later before any pioneers arrived east of the Cascade Mountains. In addition, the journey over the Oregon Trail was for young people. Very few older people made the arduous journey.

Some of the pioneers born before 1800 were very important in the early history of Oregon. Others are nearly unknown.

LEVI SCOTT was born on February 8, 1797 in Illinois. His father died when he was very young. When his mother remarried, his step-father insisted that Levi become an indentured servant, essentially a type of slavery for a specified period of time. He only went to school for parts of three years.

Levi Scott married Edy Ennis on March 18, 1817. They first lived near Edwardsville, Illinois. They had ten children, two dying at birth. They moved to Iowa in 1834. Levi fought in the Black Hawk War. Edy died of typhoid fever in 1842.

Levi and son, John Morgan Scott, decided to move to Oregon in 1844, the second year of the Oregon Trail. The other children were left behind with relatives. Levi was elected captain of the wagon train beyond Fort Laramie. After spending the winter at Oregon City, Levi and John settled near Dallas. Levi became a very good friend of Jesse Applegate and spent the winter of 1845-46 with the Applegate family.

Levi went with the Applegates in 1846 when they discovered the route which became known as the Applegate Trail. Levi actually led the first immigrants over this route. His son, William was one of the immigrants of 1846. Levi also led the pioneers over the Applegate Trail in 1847. Three of Daniel Boone's grandsons were in that party.

The Scotts took up claims near Yoncalla in 1848. About 1850, Levi founded the town of Scottsburg at the head of navigation on the Umpqua River. This port town supplied southern Oregon and northern California. Levi set up a sawmill and a newspaper at Scottsburg.

Levi was elected to be a representative to the Oregon Territorial Council from 1852-1854 and later to the Oregon Constitutional Convention. But, Levi was restless and went to the gold mines in Idaho for a time. At the age of 73, he bought cattle and settled near Tygh Valley south of The Dalles. After the terrible winter of 1874, only 500 cattle out of over 2000 still survived. He was essentially broke, and for a year, he became the caretaker of the grounds and buildings of the University of Oregon.

After John Scott's wife, Claressa, died, he drove a herd of cattle across the Cascade Mountains and settled in the Agency Valley near Beulah, north of the present hamlet of Juntura. Levi soon followed. John's son, Levi, Jr., died of tuberculosis at the Agency Valley ranch. In 1889, John and Levi took a trip to Klamath Falls. There Levi met his daughter, Mary Jane, who had lost contact with her father for nearly 40 years. She and her husband operated a ranch near Ashland.

Levi Scott died of pneumonia on April 21, 1890 and is buried in the Beulah Cemetery north of Juntura. He and Levi Scott, Jr. share a nine foot white obelisk. In the same cemetery, lies John Scott and Nancy Scott Shelton, another of Levi's daughters. Nancy and her husband ran a ranch near Baker, but she spent a part of each year at Beulah. The largest monument to Levi Scott is Mt. Scott at Crater Lake. The mountain is named for Levi.

STEPHEN CARROLL was born in 1793. He fought in the War of 1812 and was captured by the British. He also fought in the Black Hawk War as part of the 2 Regiment, Ohio Militia. He came to Oregon in 1849. In 1868 he settled on Bridge Creek near the present Painted Hills National Monument. With him was his son, Samuel Carroll and Samuel's wife, Margaret.

On June 2, 1884, a flash flood down Bridge Creek destroyed much of the town of Mitchell. This flood drowned Nancy (Carroll) Wilson and three of her children, Autia (the oldest boy who died trying to rescue others), Maggie, and baby George. Nancy was the daughter of Samuel and Margaret Carroll. Two of the Wilson children survived, ten year old Julia and Clyde. The nearest neighbor, Christian Meyer, was miles away. Julia had to walk to the Meyer place alone as her father was away from home, and Clyde was not found until the next day.

Stephen Carroll is buried in the Carroll Cemetery near the Painted Hills. He has two tombstones. The stone placed by a great grandson in 1969 states that he died in 1886. A tombstone placed by the U.S. Government in 1971 claims that Stephen died in 1883.

JOSEPH LAVADOUR was born in 1791 and died October 13, 1892. He lived to be 101 years old. He was a fur trader in western Oregon as early as 1825. He lived on the South Umpqua River for many years. Lavadoure Creek in Douglas County is named for him. (Note the e on the name of the Creek.) It is not known when he came to the Umatilla Indian Reservation. He probably was a French-Canadian. His wife, Lisette, was born in 1817 and died January 21, 1891. She probably was an Indian. The Lavadours are buried in the St. Andrews Mission Cemetery on the Umatilla Indian Reservation near Pendleton.

NANCY PRICE was born on April 20, 1799. She died January 17, 1889. Her husband **WILLIAM A. PRICE** was born on April 28, 1806 and died on April 17, 1892. They are buried in the Weston Cemetery.

NANCY STONE was born on February 3, 1793, and died on August 16, 1874. She is buried in the Kees Cemetery near Weston. Her tombstone, like many of the tombstones in this cemetery, has been destroyed by vandals and is broken into three pieces.

ELIZABETH MANSFIELD was born in 1796. She died on May 20, 1884 at an age of 87 years, 6 months, and 3 days. She too is in the Kees Cemetery, and her tombstone has been broken.

JOSEPH NICHOLS was born January 19, 1798 in Virginia. In the early 1800's during a flood, the family was adrift on a raft that capsized. Only Joe and a brother survived. His wife was Indiana Nichols. They moved to California in 1876 to join son Joseph Nichols, Jr. In 1878 they came to a mile north of the present town of Bonanza. In 1880, Joe, Sr. built a log cabin for Joe, Jr. and his wife, Mary. The cabin still stands and is in the Bonanza Cemetery today. Joe, Sr. died November 18, 1898 at the age of 100 years, 9 months, and 29 days. He was the second person to be buried in the Bonanza Cemetery.

PETER ZELL was born in 1795 and died February 12, 1881. Little is known about Peter, but the obituary of his son, Peter Zell, Jr. gives some clues. The son was born in Indiana and crossed the plains in 1864 to the Willamette Valley. He settled at Prineville in 1879. Peter Zell is buried in the Prineville Cemetery.

ROBERT THOMPSON BALDWIN was born in England on July 13, 1795. He arrived in Pennsylvania in 1830 and set up a harness trade. He moved to St. Louis in 1838. In 1856 he came to Jackson County. He opened the first harness shop in Klamath County at Bonanza. He also ran a shop in Linkville. His wife was **ISABELLA BALDWIN**, who was born December 18, 1820. Robert died June 21, 1889. (His tombstone gives the date June 24.) Isabella died November 21, 1897. They are in the Klamath Falls Cemetery. They were the parents of Wallace Baldwin.

JEMIMA SIANDEKER (Spelling not certain) was born in 1797. She died February 11, 1879, aged 82 years, 3 months, and ? days. Nothing is known about her except what is on her tombstone in the Ballow (Valley) Cemetery on Ballow Road near Milton-Freewater. Her tombstone is a slab broken into three pieces and lying on the ground.

DAVID HARER was born in December 1799. He died June 17, 1883, aged 83 years, 6 months. Nothing is known about David except what is on his tombstone in the Ballow Cemetery near Milton-Freewater. His tombstone is a concrete slab which is broken and lying on the ground.

Chapter 3
Victims Of The Bannock War

The Bannock War occurred during June and July, 1878. Bannock and some Paiute Indians went on the war path across southern Idaho and crossed into southeastern Oregon. They travelled north near Riley and the John Day River region. The Indians suffered a major defeat by General O. O. Howard's troops south of Pilot Rock. They tried to retreat by roughly the same route that they used on their way north. This was the last major Indian uprising in Oregon.

About 2000 Indians took part in the Bannock War. It has been estimated that 78 Indians were killed. Only nine soldiers were killed, but 31 civilians died. We have tried to locate the graves of the civilians without success.

JAMES R. DAULBY was born in Baltimore, Maryland. He was killed in June 1878 by Indians in Grant County. He was 23 years old and is buried in the Canyon City Cemetery.

ELMER OLIVER ALDRICH was born on August 11, 1859. Apparently, he and several civilian friends decided to look for the hostile Indians who were moving through the John Day River country. They found the Indians, and Aldrich was killed on Murderers Creek south of Dayville on June 29, 1878. He is buried on a knoll south of the John Day River a few miles east of Dayville along the pioneer road between The Dalles and Canyon City. The grave is south of US 26 on a State of Oregon Wildlife Reserve.

JOHN VEY was born about 1836. He and his brothers, Joseph and Tony, purchased the famous Vey Ranch on Butter Creek from the Ayre brothers in the 1870's. John was killed by Indians on July 5, 1878 while herding sheep on Camas Prairie near Ukiah. He was 42 years old. He is buried in the Pilot Rock Cemetery.

As the Indians were approaching the Pilot Rock area, sheriff J. L. Sperry organized a group of 53 volunteers from Pendleton and Pilot Rock to fight them. While they were eating lunch at Willow Spring south of Pilot Rock near the present Battle Mountain State Park, they were attacked by about 150 or more Indians. Two of the volunteers were killed and several were wounded. The volunteers finally escaped at night.

HARRISON HALE was killed during the escape from Willow Spring on the night of July 6, 1878. He was 38 years old. One of Portland's mayors, Bud Clark, is a descendant of Harrison Hale. He is buried in the Pleasant Point Cemetery on the Currin Ranch near Lena in Morrow County.

CHARLES L. JEWELL was a State Senator. He had a large band of sheep at Camas Prairie. As he was going to investigate how his sheep were doing, he was wounded by Indians on July 6. He hid in the brush for three days before he was found. He died July 12, 1878 in Pendleton. He is buried in the Olney Cemetery in Pendleton.

GEORGE COGGAN was 48 years old when he was killed by Indians on July 12, 1878 near Cayuse Station east of Pendleton. He is buried in the Olney Cemetery in Pendleton.

T. B. SMITH and **JAMES MYERS** share a seven foot obelisk as their final resting place in the Union Cemetery. They were freighters who were killed by Indians on July 12, 1878 at Deadman Pass. Smith was aged 27 years, 6 months and 15 days. Myers was 45 years of age. Deadman Pass is along Interstate Highway 84 between LaGrande and Pendleton.

Chapter 4

Pioneers Of The Dalles Area

NATHAN OLNEY was the first permanent white settler at The Dalles. In 1847 he established a trading post there. He sold merchandise to the Indians and to the pioneers coming over the Oregon Trail. Captain Nathan Olney came to Oregon in 1845 in the same wagon train as Joel Palmer and Samuel Barlow. He was made a captain in the Cayuse War of 1848. He fought with Colonel Cornelius Gilliam, who was accidently killed in that war. Nathan went to California for a short time in 1849. He sold his store in 1852 and established a ferry at the mouth of the Deschutes River to transport immigrants across the river. This made him the first settler in what later became Sherman County. He raised stock and operated a store at Fairbanks on the Oregon Trail in 1853. Later, he moved to Fivemile Creek near The Dalles and raised stock. In 1854 he became the first justice of the peace in Wasco County. He was deputy sheriff in 1855. He was the U.S. Indian Agent of the Oregon Territory from 1854 to 1859. He was a guide and fought in the Yakima Indian War of 1856. He was made city marshall of The Dalles in 1864.

Nathan Olney's wife was Annette Hallacoola (or Hallicola), an Indian princess. He eventually left her and married a white woman. This marriage did not last, so he married Annette again, in 1859. Nathan was born in 1824. He died in 1866 from an infected wound caused by an Indian arrow. He is buried at Fort Simcoe, Washington. His tombstone is surrounded by a wooden fence. A plaque tells part of his life's story.

EDWARD CRATE was born in Canada in 1810 or 1821. He came to Fort Vancouver in 1836. He carried mail and freight between the various Hudsons Bay Company's posts by pack train. In 1848 he fought Indians after the Whitman Massacre. He came to The Dalles in 1849 and became the second settler in Wasco County when he took up a land claim. He married SOPHIA BOUCHER in 1844, and they had 14 children. He died in 1894. Sophia was born in 1818 or 1830 and died in 1911. The Crates are buried in St. Peters Cemetery in The Dalles.

WILLIAM C. LAUGHLIN and wife, MARY LAUGHLIN arrived at The Dalles in 1850. They bought worn out cattle from the immigrants coming over the Oregon Trail. The next year they would sell these cattle to new immigrants at a good profit. They also sold eggs and garden vegetables to the tired immigrants. In 1852 they started a store at Fairbanks on the Oregon Trail in partnership with Frank Camp. In 1860 they bought the famous Oregon House hotel in The Dalles.

William C. Laughlin was born December 27, 1814 and died on September 7, 1864. Mary was born on January 28, 1818 and died on January 17, 1898. They are buried in The Dalles IOOF Cemetery.

WENTWORTH LORD was born in Maine in 1832. He came to The Dalles in 1858 and ran a store. He became president of the Wasco Warehouse Company which dealt in wool, hides, and grain. He guided the development of an electric plant on the White River and ran a power line to The Dalles.

Mr. Lord married ELIZABETH LAUGHLIN. She was born in Missouri in 1841. She came to The Dalles in 1850 with her parents, William C. and Mary (Yeargin) Laughlin. Wentworth died in 1917 and Elizabeth in 1913. They are buried with her parents in an enclosure in The Dalles IOOF Cemetery.

ORLANDO HUMASON was born in Ohio in 1828. He crossed the plains to California during the gold rush of 1849. Later, he went to Champoeg,

Oregon. In 1853 he arrived in The Dalles and worked in a Hudson's Bay Company Store. He was in the State Legislature for three terms where he introduced the bill to establish Wasco County in 1853. Thus, he is often referred to as "the father of Wasco County." He helped establish the government of The Dalles. In 1855 he was made a captain of Dalles Company B, and he served in the Yakima Indian War in 1856. He built a 270 foot boat that operated between the mouth of the Deschutes River and Wallula in 1857. He was one of the organizers of The Dalles To Deschutes Portage Freight And Passenger Company which operated from 1857 to 1863. This company was formed to get freight from the Dalles to above Celilo Falls by way of Company Hollow. Humason was elected a county judge in 1858.

He married **PHOEBE (or PHEBE) JACKSON** in 1857. She was the daughter of Jonathan Jackson, who ran a sawmill at Dufur. She married a Mr. Dekum after Orlando died in 1875. She was born in 1840 and died in 1920. She and Orlando are buried with other Humasons in The Dalles IOOF Cemetery. A huge obelisk towers over the Humason graves.

THE SNIPES FAMILY. The Snipes family was in North Carolina before 1835. They moved to Tennessee in 1837 and on to Iowa in 1847. The parents were **ELAM SNIPES,** who was born in 1810, and **ASENATH SNIPES,** who was born in 1812. (On their tombstone, Elam is given as Elem, and Asenath is listed as Asenith.)

One son, **GEORGE R. SNIPES,** was born in 1832. He fell in love with **MARTHA IMBLER,** but her father, Dave Imbler, did not approve. The Imblers left for Oregon in the 1850's to get away from George. George learned of this and took after his sweetheart in another wagon train. Near Dufur, south of The Dalles, Martha was able to escape and elope with George. The young couple lived in The Dalles, until 1854 when they settled at Rowena. Trouble with the Indians forced them to move to The Dalles again in 1862. George and Martha had a prosperous life and 14 children. He died in 1922 and she in 1901. They are buried in The Dalles IOOF Cemetery.

BEN SNIPES, another son of Elam and Asenath, was born in 1835. He crossed the plains to Oregon at the age of 17 as part of the George Humphrey wagon train in 1852. He took a pack train from Salem to California where he sold apples for a dollar a pound. He mined for gold and ran a butcher shop. He then went to the Fraser River mines in Canada. An Indian showed Ben the great grass lands of the Yakima Valley. In 1855, he went into partnership with John Jeffries. They bought cattle and fattened them in the Yakima Valley. The cattle were trailed to the Kamloops area where they were sold to miners at a great profit. Soon Ben was the largest cattleman in the Northwest. At one time he had 125,000 head of cattle and 20,000 horses. His home was in The Dalles, but his ranching headquarters was at Sunnyside in the Yakima Valley.

Ben married **MARY PARROTT,** who had arrived in Oregon in 1847 with John Golden's party. The Goldens founded Goldendale, Washington. Ben and Mary became very wealthy. About 1887, they moved to Seattle where he bought much land. He started 2 banks, one being in Ellensburg. He was forced into bankruptcy during the panic of 1893. A son, Ben Snipes, Jr. was born in 1870. He took a ship for Alaska in 1891, but the ship disappeared and nothing was ever found of it. Ben Snipes died January 12, 1906 and Mary A. Snipes on March 25, 1920. Their tombstones are marked by a monument in The Dalles IOOF Cemetery.

The parents, Elam and Asenath Snipes came to Oregon in 1863 where they took over the property at Rowena. Later, they moved to near Goldendale, Washington where they became successful cattle ranchers. Elam died in 1892 and Asenath in 1894. They are buried on top of Snipes Butte, a few miles southwest of Goldendale. A six foot moss-covered natural rock marks their grave. To reach the monument, a hike of a mile across pasture land is required.

MARTHA SNIPES was a daughter of Elam and Asenath. She married **JAMES O. LYLE,** the founder of Lyle, Washington. She died on August 9, 1887, aged 53 years, 9 months, 9 days. James Lyle was born in Pennsylvania in 1831. He moved to Indiana and Iowa before going to California by ox team in 1853. He returned to Iowa and married Martha in

1857. They came west in 1863. The Lyles are buried in Lyle, Washington.

MILO M. CUSHING was born in New York in 1820. He was in the Mexican War. He came to The Dalles in 1852 as a sergeant in the army. He started a store in 1853 and then the Cushing House Hotel, maybe the first hotel in The Dalles. He sold out in 1858 and started farming on Fifteen Mile Creek. He was the first presidential appointed postmaster of The Dalles (then called Wascopam) in 1859. Milo married **MARY PIGGOTT** in 1854, the first wedding after Wasco County was established. She was born on June 11, 1834. She went to New York and then crossed the plains in 1852 as the care taker of Major O. G. Haller's children. Milo died in 1906 and Mary on November 18, 1925. She, and other Cushings, are buried in St. Peters Cemetery in The Dalles.

JACOB JUKER was born in 1820. He fought in the Mexican War. When he came to The Dalles, he ran a cigar store. He was appointed postmaster by President Lincoln. He died in 1869 and was buried in the Masonic Cemetery in The Dalles. The Masonic Cemetery has been destroyed, and his tombstone has been lost. The pioneers buried in the Masonic Cemetery are now remembered only by their names placed on a monument in another cemetery south of The Dalles.

COLONEL NATHANIEL GATES was born in 1814 in Virginia. He came to The Dalles as a lawyer in 1854. He surveyed the site of The Dalles and built the Gates Hotel, which may have been the first in the town. He was a veteran of the Yakima War in 1855. He was mayor of The Dalles four times between 1865 and 1878. He was speaker of the house in the State Legislature in 1859 and was State Senator in 1857. He has been called "the father of The Dalles." His wife was **CATHERINE GATES**, who lived from 1828 to 1901. Nathaniel died on May 20, 1889. They are buried in The Dalles IOOF Cemetery.

The **FRENCH FAMILY** members were bankers and prominent residents of The Dalles. **DANIEL M. FRENCH** was born in Vermont on June 16, 1828. He arrived in The Dalles in 1862 and ran a general store. Later, he went into the banking business. He

headed the giant Gilman-French Land and Livestock Company of Eastern Oregon by furnishing the money to buy the livestock for its various ranches. He married **ALLIE M. GEE** in 1865. She died January 13, 1875 at 40 years of age. He died January 2, 1902. They are buried in the French enclosure with its tall obelisk in The Dalles IOOF Cemetery.

SMITH FRENCH was a brother of Daniel. He was born on March 26, 1837 and died February 27, 1919. His wife, **ESTHER B. FRENCH** was born December 5, 1838 and died on April 6, 1924. Smith French managed the Gilman-French Land and Livestock Company for a while. **JOSHUA W. FRENCH** was another brother. He was born on September 13, 1830 in Holland, Vermont and died December 23, 1907. His wife, **LAURA ELLEN (BURKE) FRENCH,** was born on May 25, 1840 and died on October 28, 1923. All of these people are buried in the French enclosure.

MARSHALL FRENCH was another brother. He was born October 6, 1844 and died April 25, 1911. For some reason, he is buried outside the French enclosure at The Dalles IOOF Cemetery.

DR. POLHEMUS CRAIG came with an army unit to The Dalles in 1852. He had been a surgeon in the Mexican War. Later, he became a druggist. His wife, **ANN ELIZABETH CRAIG** was an army nurse. He died November 12, 1877 at an age of 67 years. She died November 12, 1894, aged 74 years. They are buried in St Peters Cemetery in The Dalles.

ZELICK M. DONNELL married **CAMILLA THOMSON** in 1852, and they crossed the plains to Oregon on their honeymoon. She walked the length of the Oregon Trail. In 1858 they moved with their cattle from the Brownsville area to The Dalles and settled on Fifteenmile Creek near Freebridge. Zelick was a state senator in 1864. He was born in 1829 and died in 1873. She was born in 1827 and died in 1914. They are buried in The Dalles IOOF Cemetery.

FREDERICK HOMER BALCH (Homer to his friends) was one of Oregon's greatest authors. His most famous book was *Bridge Of The Gods.* Indian legend says that there once was a bridge across the Columbia River at Cascade Locks. Geological evidence supports the legend. A great landslide once dammed the river and formed a lake behind the slide. Before Bonneville Dam was built, the rocks of the slide were visible in the river. Trees drowned by the lake could be seen in the river. The author remembers seeing some of the stumps of the trees in the 1930's. Radiocarbon dating of the trees gives a date for the slide as about 1260 A.D. Balch's book is woven around the Indian legend.

Balch was born in 1861 at Lebanon, Oregon. He was a preacher as well as a writer. His sweetheart was **GENEVRA WHITCOMB** of The Dalles. They had some kind of a spat, so they never married. She was born July 9, 1866 and died at The Dalles on January 29, 1886. Balch was the minister at her funeral. Balch wrote a novel in her memory. Balch died on June 3, 1891, possibly of tuberculosis. He is buried in the Lyle, Washington Cemetery. Two stones mark his grave inside an enclosure. Genevra Whitcomb is buried a few feet away with her parents.

Balch's mother was **HARRIET SNIDER**. She walked all the way across the plains in 1852. She married James Anderson Balch. There is an unmarked stone beside Homer Balch's grave. This is said to mark the grave of Harriet.

LOUIS SCHOLL was born in Carlsruhe, Germany on November 4, 1829. He arrived in the United States in 1848. He went by oxen to California in 1852 and then on to Oregon. He spent much of his life working for the army as a guide, map maker, draftsman, and clerk. He was stationed at The Dalles from 1856 to 1859. While he was there, he drew up the architectural plans for Fort Dalles, Fort Simcoe, Fort Walla Walla, and Fort Colville. In 1859 he was a guide and map maker for Captain Henry D. Wallen's expedition from The Dalles to the Harney Valley. He named the valley in honor of General William S. Harney. In 1862, he was in Washington, D.C. as a secretary for Senator James Nesmith of Oregon. When the Civil War started, he was put in charge of getting ships to transport soldiers from Annapolis. He contracted pneumonia at the battle of Fredericksburg. In 1863, he returned to The Dalles. In 1864 he married **ELIZABETH FULTON**, daughter of the famous James Fulton. She was born in 1842 or 1843 in Missouri. They had three sons, Louis Jr., Bismark, and Carl. In 1877,

Scholl was a quartermaster clerk for the army at Fort Boise. He made a map for General O. O. Howard that was used in capturing Chief Joseph's band on their flight to Canada in 1877. Scholl returned to The Dalles in 1879 and went into the flour milling business.

Louis Scholl died in 1911 at the age of 82. Elizabeth died in 1915. They are buried in the Wasco Sunrise Cemetery beside a large Scholl monument.

FRANCIS (FRANK) A. SEUFERT was born in 1853 in New York. He went to California in 1882 and then to The Dalles where he bought a cannery in 1884. He developed a very large business by catching salmon with fish wheels for his cannery. He planted the first cherry orchard in The Dalles area. He became one of the most influential citizens of the area and was a mayor of The Dalles. He married **ANNIE ISABELL SCHICK**. She was born in 1855 and died in 1928. Frank died in 1929. Two large tombstones at the foot of the impressive Seufert monument mark their graves in The Dalles IOOF Cemetery.

COL. N. B. SINNOTT was born in County Wexford, Ireland. He died on October 1897 at an age of 65 years. His wife was born on February 22, 1843 and died November 30, 1902. He became a partner in the famous Umatilla House in the Dalles in 1860. Their son, **NICHOLAS J. SINNOTT**, was born in 1870 and died in 1929. He was justice of the U.S. Federal Court and a U.S. Congressman from 1913 to 1928. All these Sinnotts share a common monument in The Dalles St. Peters Cemetery.

DANIEL HANDLEY was N. B. Sinnott's partner in operating the Umatilla House. He was born in Eniscorthy County, Oxford, Ireland on February 21, 1830. He died on November 19, 1891. He married **CATHERINE BYRNE**, who died on August 20, 1906 at an age of 79 years. They are buried close to the Sinnotts in The Dalles St. Peters Cemetery.

REV. EZRA FISHER was born January 6, 1800 in Massachusetts. He was ordained as a preacher in 1830. He preached in Vermont before moving to Astoria in 1846 where he built a log church and a meeting house. He went to California during the gold rush of 1849 and made $1200. In 1850 he started a school in the Baptist Church in Oregon City. He was co-founder of Oregon City College. He homesteaded near The Dalles in 1861. Every Sunday he walked the four miles to The Dalles to preach. In 1874 he was elected superintendent of the schools of Wasco County. He died of pneumonia on November 1, 1874 and is buried in The Dalles Pioneer Cemetery.

The Moody family was very important in the history of The Dalles. Zenas Ferry Moody not only had businesses in the town, but he also was a governor of Oregon. His son, **MALCOLM MOODY**, was born in 1854 and died in 1925. Malcolm was a congressman, a warehouse operator, and a rancher. He was mayor of The Dalles in 1889 and '90. He also ran a toll bridge on the Deschutes River until 1922. **WILLIAM H. MOODY** was another son of Zenas Moody. He ran a warehouse at The Dalles and at Shaniko. William was born October 5, 1860 and died on June 14, 1919. Malcolm and William are buried in The Dalles IOOF Cemetery.

Chapter 5

Wasco County Pioneers

LEWIS PAYETTE HENDERSON settled on Fifteenmile Creek a few miles above Dufur in 1852. He was the first in the area. His wife was ZYLPHAE (or ZYLPHA) E. HENDERSON. Their son, GEORGE, was killed by a runaway team on April 17, 1879, aged 15 years, 2 months, and 13 days. The mother died on April 17, 1875, aged 30 years, 11 days. The family is buried in the Henderson Cemetery near Dufur. There is an unmarked stone beside Zylpha's tombstone that is said to mark the grave of Lewis.

WILLIAM R. MENEFEE was born in Virginia on December 5, 1823. He came to Oregon in the great migration of 1852 and settled in Yamhill County. He came to Dufur in 1855 and farmed. Later he ran a store and built the Menefee-Dufur Fort. He built the first water system for Dufur and was a justice of peace for eight years. His wife was NANCY JANE MENEFEE, who was born October 30, 1831 and died February 11, 1907. William died June 19, 1906. They share a common tombstone in the Dufur IOOF Cemetery.

THOMAS W. S. SLUSHER was born in Pennsylvania in 1847. He fought in the Civil War in Co. 22, Reg. Penn. Vol. Cavalry, at the age of 13. He moved to Oregon and taught in the Willamette Valley. Later, he settled above Dufur. He was Wasco County's surveyor in 1872. He married ARABELLE H. DUFUR, the daughter of Andrew and Lois Dufur, in 1878. The town of Dufur was named for her parents. She was born in Wisconsin on July 13, 1856. Her family moved to Portland when she was three. She came to Dufur in 1872. Thomas died on April 3, 1890. Arabelle then married WILLIAM H. STAATS in 1900. Mr. Staats was born on January 9, 1867 in Aurora, Oregon. The Staats moved to Maupin, which they named, in 1910. They ran the post office and the first store in Maupin. They remained in Maupin until 1935 when they retired to Dufur. Arabelle died May 7, 1939 and William in 1943. Thomas, Arabelle, and William are all buried in the Henderson Cemetery.

HORACE RICE was born in Ohio in 1829. He came to the Willamette Valley in 1851. In 1863 he came to Rice, which is near Dufur and Boyd. He may have been the first person to plant wheat on the highlands above Fifteenmile Creek. He married ELIZA J. BOLTON in 1849. She was born in 1830 and died in 1915. Horace also died in 1915. They are buried in The Dalles IOOF Cemetery under a large tombstone.

ABSALOM D. BOLTON and DANIEL BOLTON came to Oregon in 1851 with the Rice family. They nearly starved to death on the Oregon Trail. In 1863 they settled east of Rice. Absalom was born in Virginia in 1821. His wife was OLIVE BOLTON, who died February 19, 1918 at an age of 85 years, 5 months, 13 days. Absalom died on February 20, 1903, aged 81 years, 18 days. Their grave in the Rice Cemetery is marked by a white monument five and a half feet tall.

Daniel Bolton moved to near Boyd. He married ELIZABETH J. FULLWEILDER. Their son, Wilbur Daniel Bolton, was born in Boyd in 1860. In later years, Wilbur moved to Antelope and ran a store there with his brother, Virgil. Daniel Bolton was born on May 1, 1820 and died November 11, 1887. Elizabeth was born on June 15, 1830, and she died on August 22, 1897. They are buried in The Dalles IOOF Cemetery.

SYLVESTER W. MASON was born on July 12, 1841 in New York. He went to California by train in 1869. He homesteaded at Boyd in 1870. He married LYDIA O. KEITH, who was born on July 7, 1853. Sylvester died on May 19, 1922, and Lydia died on June 2, 1924. Their grave in the Rice Cemetery is marked by a large granite monument.

JOHN MASON came to Boyd with his brother, Sylvester. He was born on March 3, 1824. He married Mary Masouart (or Masquert) of Rice. Her father may have been **NICHOLAS MASOUART**, who was born in France on November 2, 1836. He died on January 14, 1911. John Mason died on June 7, 1890. John and Nicholas are buried in the Rice Cemetery.

CHARLES H. SOUTHERN was born in Iowa in 1855. He came to Boyd in 1871. In 1878 he married **EMMA A. RICE**, daughter of Horace Rice. Charles laid out the town of Boyd in 1895, and he ran a mercantile business there in 1899. Charles died in 1935. Emma, who was born in 1856, died in 1946. They are buried in the Rice Cemetery.

Apparently, the parents of Charles Southern were **MARTIN SOUTHERN** and **ELIZABETH A. SOUTHERN**. Martin was born on December 24, 1817 and died on November 8, 1877. Elizabeth was born on December 25, 1828 and died on May 5, 1900. They also are buried in Rice Cemetery, their graves being marked by a six foot monument.

WILLIAM L. WARD was born on March 26, 1826. He crossed the plains in 1859 to Dufur. In 1860 he became one of the first settlers on Eightmile Creek. He built the first school there. He also ran a sawmill. He left for seven years and then returned to Ward Hill near Boyd in 1873. He married **HANNA H. POTTS**, who was born on November 27, 1831. William died on December 28, 1897, and she died on November 20, 1909. A large moss-covered monument in the trees marks their grave in the Dufur IOOF Cemetery.

JOSEPH HAYNES was born in Massachusetts on December 14, 1826. He fought in the Civil War. He came to Oregon in 1879 and farmed near Boyd. He married **LUCINDA FREEMAN** in 1853. She was born on March 12, 1831. They retired to Dufur in 1898. Joe died February 27, 1908, and Lucinda died March 20, 1915. They are buried in the Dufur IOOF Cemetery.

JACOB CRAFT was born on June 25, 1819 in Virginia. His family moved to Ohio in 1838. He fought in the Mexican War, and during the Civil War he trained recruits. He married **ROSANNA** (**ROSE ANNA** on tombstone) **DECKER** in 1852. They came to Boyd in 1883. Jacob died on February 15, 1906. She died on September 12, 1899, aged 64 years. They are buried in the Dufur IOOF Cemetery.

THOMAS ANGELL was born on May 7, 1810. He settled two miles below Dufur in 1860 but moved to Eightmile Creek in 1861 or 1864 to farm. He had crossed the plains to California in 1849. He returned to the East and married **SUSAN PENNY** in 1850. She was born May 12, 1832. They took the Oregon Trail to Lebanon in 1852. Their son, Homer, was a lawyer, a member of the State Legislature, and a U.S. Congressman. He was born in 1875. Thomas died November 26, 1888, and Susan died December 27, 1928. They are buried in the Eightmile Cemetery.

Robert Mays was born on October 25, 1830. His wife, Lodema Mays was born on September 28, 1833. They crossed the plains in 1852 and settled in Benton County. They came to Dufur in 1858 and moved to Tygh Valley in 1862. In 1865, they returned to Dufur. The Mays owned five ranches where they raised thousands of cattle. Robert was also a blacksmith.

John Y. Todd built a bridge across the Deschutes River near Sherars Falls in 1860. Robert Mays was a partner in this toll road operation, which was later taken over by Joseph Sherar. This road became a very important route to Central Oregon and the mines at Canyon City. In 1862, Mays took over the operation of the toll road and bridge.

The Mays moved to The Dalles in 1902. He died on April 7, 1902 and Lodema on December 23, 1910. Their graves are marked by stones beside a large Mays monument.

JOSEPH H. SHERAR was born November 16, 1833 in Vermont. He went to California in 1855. In 1862 he took a pack train loaded with supplies for the miners at Canyon City. This proved to be a very profitable operation, so in 1871 he bought the toll road and bridge across the Deschutes River for $7,040. He greatly improved the road for 30 miles on each side of the river. The road became known as Sherars Road. It is very important in the history of transportation east of the Cascade Mountains.

Remnants of Sherars Road still exist with giant rock walls across gullies and hillsides. It still is one of the most interesting pioneer roads in Oregon. Sections of it make an excellent hiking trail. Joe built a 33 room hotel at the bridge as well as a large barn.

Joe married **JANE A. HERBERT** in 1863. She was the daughter of one of the first settlers in Tygh Valley. She was born October 11, 1848. The Sherars built the first flour mill in the area at the White River Falls. They also filed on a homestead in a canyon along their road west of Sherars Falls. Jane Sherar died on July 8, 1907 and Joe on February 11, 1908. They share a simple tombstone in The Dalles IOOF Cemetery.

The Butlers were early settlers in Tygh Valley. Daniel Webster Butler came to the valley in 1856 or 1858 and established the first store at Tygh Valley. His brothers, **JONATHAN BUTLER** and **POLK BUTLER**, also settled in Tygh Valley. Jonathan was born October 12, 1831 in Illinois and died on February 26, 1891. His wife, **MARY ANN BUTLER** was born on November 13, 1843 and died on July 17, 1901. Polk Butler was born on September 25, 1846, and he died March 12, 1907. His wife, **DELPHINE BUTLER,** was born July 15, 1846 and died March 4, 1914. US Highway 197 leaves Tygh Valley for Tygh Ridge by Butler Canyon, which is named after the Butler families. The Jonathan and Polk Butler families are buried in the Dufur IOOF Cemetery.

WILLIAM MILTON McCORKLE was born in Indiana on February 25, 1828 or 1829. He went to California in 1849 or 1850 and became wealthy. He returned to Indiana and then came to Linn County in 1852 by a horse team. He moved to Dufur in 1872. He built a flour mill at Tygh Valley. His second marriage was to **ABBY ZUMWALT,** who was born in 1840. William died in 1910 and Abby in 1919. They are buried in the Tygh Valley Cemetery near the sawmill.

WILLIAM HEISLER was born in Pennsylvania in 1828. He fought in the Mexican War in 1848. He moved to California in 1849 to mine. He returned to Missouri in 1851 and married **MARTHA McCONNELL,** who was born in 1834. They came to Salem in 1852. They moved to Prineville in 1870 and started a store in the new town in 1871. William was Prineville's first postmaster. The Heislers returned to The Dalles in 1880. They moved to Dufur in 1882 and ran a store. They sold out in 1886 and returned to Crook County where they raised cattle and ran the Heisler Stage Station on Hay Creek. In 1897 they returned to Dufur and operated a flour mill until 1903. William died on August 14, 1904, and Martha died on August 8, 1925. They are buried in the Dufur IOOF Cemetery. The Heisler home in Dufur still stands.

RICHARD BURREL SANFORD married **NANCY BARBARETTE CORUM.** Richard was born on October 24, 1827 in Kentucky. Nancy was born on December 24, 1829. Her father had been a large slave holder. The Sanfords arrived at Wamic after 1876. Richard had lost track of his mother, and she had remarried a Corum also. Richard found his mother living in Wamic! Nancy's sister **MINERVA ANNE CORUM** was born on April 13, 1812. She had taught school near the mouth of the Deschutes River. Richard died on August 1, 1911, Nancy on June 16, 1918, and Minerva on November 20, 1896. All of these pioneers are buried in the Lone Pine (Wamic) Cemetery a few miles from the town of Wamic. All their names are engraved on the same large monument. Also, on this monument is the name **MARY BARBOT CORUM,** who was born on May 9, 1801 and who died February 19, 1891. Mary's maiden name was Masquerier, and she was born in Paris, Kentucky. She married Hiram Corum, Sr. Mary was the mother of Nancy B. (Corum) Sanford and Minerva Corum.

LOUIS J. KLINGER was born in Missouri on October 19, 1837. He arrived in Oregon by the Barlow Road in 1847. He married **MELISSA J. WOODCOCK** in 1861. She was born in 1844. They settled on Eightmile Creek in 1863. He freighted between The Dalles and Boise for ten years or more. Louis and John Doyle brought the first wheat separator to Wasco County. The Klingers retired to Dufur in 1899 where he was a mayor. Louis died in 1915 and Melissa in 1927. They are buried in the Dufur IOOF Cemetery.

JOHN M. ROTH was born in 1839 in Germany. He came to Wisconsin in 1856. He fought in the

Civil War. He married **MARGARET UNSEL.** In 1875 they became early settlers at Kingsley, a town south of Dufur. John died in 1924. Margaret was born in 1850 and died in 1916. They are buried in the Dufur IOOF Cemetery.

GEORGE J. FRIEND was born in 1865. His wife was **CLARA B. FRIEND,** who was born in 1873. George was a farmer and a blacksmith in Kingsley in 1898. There he built a two-story dance hall. In 1902, they moved to the town of Friend, which was named for them. George died in 1937 and Clara in 1941. They have a granite monument in the Friend Cemetery.

JOHN WESLEY RUSSELL was born on December 25, 1835 in Illinois. He was in the Civil War and participated in Sherman's March To The Sea. He married Anne Balckledge in 1886. They came to Kingsley in 1888. John died July 24, 1928. He is buried in the South Kingsley Cemetery. There is a block with a GAR star beside a large Russell monument.

WILLIAM ENDERSBY was born in 1845. He came to Oregon in 1850. He married **CORA M. FLIGG.** They moved to Eightmile Creek in 1864. The hamlet of Endersby was named for them. William was killed in an automobile accident on September 10, 1926. They are buried in the Dufur IOOF Cemetery. The dates on the tombstone seem to be incorrect.

JAMES FRANCIS MARION STEERS was born in Kentucky on March 18, 1832. He crossed the plains to the Willamette Valley in 1865. He moved to Wapinitia Flat in 1866 and then to Tygh Valley in 1867. He had been a minister. He married **ALVIRA HONORIUS** in 1854. She was born on March 4, 1836 in Illinois. James died on April 9, 1867, and Alvira married Benjamin C. McAtee. Ben was murdered in 1893 in the Grande Ronde Valley. Alvira died on March 4, 1911. James and Alvira are buried in the Tygh Valley Cemetery which is several miles northwest of the town on Badger Creek.

PHOEBE A. McATEE missed being born in the eighteenth century by one day. She was born on January 1, 1800. She was born in Kentucky. She married William R. Cantrall. This may have been her second marriage. She died on November 12, 1878 and is buried in the Tygh Valley Cemetery on Badger Creek. Her tombstone gives her last name as McAtee, which apparently was her maiden name. There is some mystery here! In the same cemetery is **W. H. McATEE,** who was born September 12, 1825 and who died on November 12, 1890. He too was born in Kentucky. He is buried with his wife. **SARAH McATEE** who was born on July 28, 1818 and died on October 24, 1898. What relationship was Phoebe to W. H. McAtee?

DR. LARKIN VANDERPOOL was born in Missouri on June 21, 1831. He came to Polk County in 1852. He married **MARY TURNAGE,** who died on March 8, 1901 at an age on 69. Larkin became a doctor by just reading books without ever going to a medical school! The Vanderpools moved to Prineville in 1869, and he was the town's first doctor. They moved to Dufur in 1883 where he became that town's first doctor. He invented the famous SB cough drops which were sold nationwide as the Smith Brothers Cough drops. Larkin died on March 24, 1894. Larkin and Mary are buried in the Dufur IOOF Cemetery.

AMOS DARNIELLE was born in Illinois on April 19, 1824. (One source says the date was September 18.) He was the captain of a wagon train that crossed the plains to Oregon City by the Barlow Road in 1865. He homesteaded near Eightmile Creek. He died on August 13, 1915 and is buried in the Eightmile Cemetery.

JONAH HARRISON MOSIER was born March 10, 1821 in Pennsylvania or Maryland. He went to Missouri in 1839. He went to California in 1849 and then to The Dalles in 1853. He married **JANE ROLLINS** in 1846. Jonah was the first building contractor in The Dalles and built a hotel for Milo Cushing. In 1854 he built a sawmill at Mosier Creek and claimed the land where the town of Mosier is today. In 1865, '67, and '68 he drove cattle to the mines in Montana. He was in the State Legislature at one time. Jane died August 28, 1865. Jonah died on September 6, 1894. Jonah, Jane, and son Benjamin share a common tombstone in the Mosier Pioneer Cemetery. This old cemetery is just east of Mosier Creek on a hill just south of US 30.

SAMUEL MITCHEL DRIVER was born in England or Ohio in 1814 or 1815. He came to the United States before 1824. He went to California in 1849 or 1850, where he was a successful miner. He returned to his home in Indiana in 1827, to Iowa in 1852 and then came to Oregon with family in 1852 or '53. He was a stockman in the Umpqua Valley. The Driver family came to Wamic in 1875. Sam died April 24, 1896 and is buried in the Wamic Lone Pine Cemetery.

JOHN M. LEDFORD was born in North Carolina on September 13, 1832. His wife was **ELIZABETH LEDFORD**, who was born on July 28, 1844. They resided in The Dalles many years before moving to Wamic. John died July 27, 1895 and Elizabeth on January 8, 1908. Each has the same type of pillar in the Wamic Lone Pine Cemetery.

HEZEKIAH STALEY was born in Virginia in 1828. He settled at Tygh Valley in 1870 and became a merchant. He was the first postmaster at Tygh Valley. He died on May 12, 1893 at an age of 65 years, 2 months, 6 days and is buried in the Wamic Lone Pine Cemetery.

JASON CUSHION DUNCAN PRATT was born on April 19, 1822. One historian claims he came West by ox team in 1859. Another historian says that he came to Oregon from Michigan by way of Panama. His wife was **AMANDA SAGE**. They settled at Tygh Valley. In 1862 the Pratts became the first settlers at what is now the town of Wamic, which at one time was called Prattsville. He was a good singer. Jason died on October 22, 1904. Amanda died on October 30, 1895, aged 68 years, 27 days. They are buried in the old Wamic Pioneer Cemetery about a quarter of a mile east of the present Wamic store. In the same cemetery is a wood marker that marks the grave of **OMAR PRATT**, who was born in 1893 and died in 1898. Only the name is still legible, but he probably was a grandson of Jason and Amanda.

JOHN END was born September 3, 1831 in England. He was a pioneer farmer in the Wamic area. He died on February 26, 1913. He has an unusual tombstone in the Wamic Lone Pine Cemetery.

GEORGE WASHINGTON LUCAS was born on October 17, 1827 in Illinois. The family moved to Missouri. Later George moved to California to mine. He married **LOUISA A. POOLE KILGORE** there in 1856. She was born in Indiana in 1835 and crossed the plains to California in 1852. In 1861 he started for the Idaho gold mines. Along the way, he may have been the first person to discover gold at Canyon City. (Other historians give credit to William Allred for discovering gold at Canyon City.) The Lucas family moved to The Dalles in 1863 where George started a tannery. Later, they moved to a farm at Wamic. "Gold fever" returned, and he mined at Greenhorn near Granite. He ran a tannery at Prairie City. When his health failed, he returned to Wamic where he died in August 1904. Louisa died in 1908. They are buried in the Wamic Lone Pine Cemetery.

THOMAS A. WARD was born in Wisconsin in 1846. He eventually came to Oregon and became the first stage driver for Henry H. Wheeler's The Dalles to Canyon City stage and express service. He settled at Cross Hollows (just south of present Shaniko) in 1864 where he ran the stage station for Henry Wheeler. Tom drove the stage from The Dalles to Cross Hollows from 1864 to 1876. He sold the stage station to August Schernakau, from which Shaniko received its name, in 1876. Tom then ran the Nansene Stage Station until 1884. Nansene was south of The Dalles on the road between The Dalles and Canyon City by way of Sherar's Bridge. Tom was the postmaster of Nansene from 1878 to 1884. He moved to The Dalles and operated a livery stable and either a store or a hotel. He was elected sheriff of Wasco County in 1892. In 1876 Tom married **MARY L. KERNS** of Grant County. Mary was born in 1854 and died in 1949. Tom died April 6, 1903. They are buried in The Dalles IOOF Cemetery.

HOWARD MAUPIN was born December 25, 1815 in Kentucky. He volunteered for the Mexican War and was stationed at Fort Leavenworth in 1846. He had moved to Missouri in 1829. He married **NANCY McCULLUM** in 1840. She was born in 1823. She too had been born in Kentucky and moved to Missouri. In 1852, the Maupins drove an ox team to near Eugene by way of the Barlow Road. Some time between 1862 and 1864, they established Maupin Station (or Old Antelope) about two miles east of present Antelope. Old Antelope was on the route to the gold mines of Canyon City from The Dalles. The station consisted of a fortified log cabin, a log barn, blacksmith shop, and corrals. Howard ran a cattle ranch while Nancy ran the station. In 1867, Howard and Jim Clark shot and killed the renegade Chief Paulina on Trout Creek. Paulina had been harassing and killing white settlers for years. The Maupins were postmasters of Old Antelope from 1871. However, Howard moved to the ranch on Trout Creek in 1872. The ranch was a few miles north of the present hamlet of Ashwood. In 1873 the Maupins sold the station to Nathan Wallace, the local blacksmith. Howard died of a stroke on January 14, 1887. Nancy died in 1906. They are buried on their Trout Creek ranch in the Maupin Cemetery. The Maupin Cemetery is also known as the Friend Cemetery. Several of their children are in this cemetery also. Nancy's grave is marked by a tombstone with only the word Mother.

ANDREW CLARNO was born in Illinois in 1820. In 1847 or 1848, he married either Eleanor Evans or Eleanor Jones. There is some confusion about her last name. ELEANOR CLARNO was born in 1825. In 1862 the Clarnos came to California by way of the Isthmus of Panama. They had been living in Illinois. In 1865 the Clarnos left California and drove a large herd of cattle to near Eugene. In 1866 Andrew scouted for land to raise stock east of the Cascade Mountains. In 1867 he drove a herd of cattle over the Scott Trail south of McKenzie Pass and settled on the west side of the John Day River about a mile north of the site of Clarno. Eleanor and their small children arrived at Clarno by way of The Dalles. The Clarnos raised hundreds of cattle and horses. Chief Paulina had stolen some of the Clarno cattle just before he was killed by Howard Maupin and Jim Clark. Eleanor died on December 7, 1897 and Andrew on January 28, 1907. The Clarnos along with several of their children and relatives are buried in the Clarno Cemetery, which is on a knoll about a mile north of the Clarno bridge on State Highway 218.

NATHAN W. WALLACE was born in Ohio in 1832. He moved to Illinois and then Iowa. He crossed the plains in 1852 to Yamhill County and then to Washington County. He married SARAH FRANCES NAUGHT in 1856. Nathan fought in the Yakima Indian War in 1856. The Wallaces moved to The Dalles in the early 1860's and ran a blacksmith shop. They lived south of Old Antelope on Current Creek before moving to Old Antelope in either 1864 or 1868. Nathan bought Maupin's Station at Old Antelope in either 1872 or '73. He was Old Antelope's first blacksmith and its second postmaster. Nathan's mother, ELIZABETH SMAILES, was living with them. She died on January 3, 1881 at the age of 74 years, 11 months, and 11 days. She is buried in the Old Antelope Cemetery. The Wallaces moved to new Antelope after 1881 where Nathan ran a blacksmith shop. He also was the postmaster and built several buildings in the new town. Nathan died September 16, 1904. Sarah, who was born on March 5, 1836, died on May 28, 1907. They are buried in the Antelope Cemetery.

HERBERT C. ROOPER was born in England in 1852. He arrived in Iowa in 1871. He came to the Antelope area in 1876 and herded sheep. He started his own ranch near Antelope in 1885 and by 1904 owned 4000 sheep and 2200 acres. He married ELIZABETH J. POHL in 1886. She had been living with the Schernakaus for whom Shaniko is named. She was born in 1866. Herbert was mayor of Antelope in 1905 and served as US land commissioner. He also published a newspaper until 1925. Herbert died in 1935 and Elizabeth in 1946. They are buried in The Dalles IOOF Cemetery.

Richard Roland Hinton was born in Missouri in 1852. By 1902 he was the largest land and sheep owner in Wasco County. He had come to the Bakeoven area when 19 years of age to start his sheep ranch. His first wife was MARY EMMA HINTON. She was born on November 22, 1852 and died February 8, 1888. Richard's second wife was MARY ANN (BIRD) HINTON. Mary was born in 1834. She was a teacher. Mary Ann shot herself to death in 1912. Both of Richard's wives are buried in the Hinton Cemetery on the Hinton-Ward Ranch near Bakeoven.

Chapter 6
Sherman County Pioneers

GEORGE MASIKER was born in New York in 1825. He crossed the plains from Illinois to Lafayette in 1852 or 1853. He lived near Yamhill until 1860 when the Masikers moved to Fifteenmile Creek near Dufur. They moved to Sand Spring in Sherman County west of Locust Grove in 1862. Here they ran a stage station which later became known as Prices Stage Station. George married PALMYRA ELIZABETH TRUMBLE in 1847. She was born in 1830 in New York. While they lived at Dufur, she taught school at Fairbanks for the Fulton children. George died in April 1863 and is buried on the hillside near Sand Spring. At first he had only a wooden marker, but some years later, his family built a domed concrete tombstone.

SAMUEL PRICE was born in 1834 in Ohio. He moved to Iowa in 1844 and then to Missouri. He came to Oregon in 1860 and lived at Dufur and Tygh Valley. He worked for George Masiker at Sand Spring. After George died, Sam married PALMYRA MASIKER in November 1864. They ran Prices Stage Station for 20 years. It was an important stage station where horses were changed on The Dalles to Salt Lake City and The Dalles to Walla Walla Stage Lines. In addition, they raised horses for the stage lines and cattle. Sand Spring produces a great deal of water in a region known for its limited supply of water. In 1884 the Prices moved to Maryhill, Washington, then to Yakima in 1891, and then to Kennewick. In 1903, they moved to Hood River, Oregon. They moved once again to Grants Pass in 1907. Palmyra died in 1917 and Sam in 1921. Their graves in Grants Pass IOOF Cemetery are marked by concrete domes on a concrete slab.

JAMES C. FULTON was born in Paoli in Orange County, Indiana on March 17, 1816. He married PRISCILLA WELLS in 1840 at Washington, Indiana. She was born in Kentucky on April 27, 1816. They lived for a while in Missouri. They came to Yamhill County by ox team in 1847. They used the Barlow Road cut-off of the Oregon Trail. James went to California in 1848 and made a fortune. He returned to Portland by boat. He was elected a colonel in the Oregon militia and took part in the Yakima War of 1856. He moved to Fairbanks east of The Dalles in 1857 and raised cattle and horses. He drove cattle to the eastern Oregon and Idaho mines for several years. He sold out in 1870 and moved to Fulton Canyon in Sherman County. He was a member of the State Legislature as well as the postmaster of Fultonville at the mouth of the Deschutes River. James died on March 15, 1896. Priscilla died on January 10, 1902. They each have a monument about nine feet tall in the Wasco Sunrise Cemetery.

The children of James and Priscilla Fulton settled in the Fulton Canyon region of Sherman County west of Wasco. Some of them became very prominent citizens of the county. JAMES FULTON, JR. was born in Missouri in 1847 and died in 1919. He married Georgia Foss. JOHN FULTON was born in 1852 and died in 1930. He was elected Sherman County judge in 1892. He also was a surveyor and rancher. His wife was BRITTANA C. GILMORE, daughter of S. M. and Martha Gilmore. Their beautiful home still is used. John and Brittana are buried in a huge vault in the Wasco Sunrise Cemetery.

ANNIE L. FULTON was born in 1860 and died in 1912. She spent most of her life with her parents. She probably was the first woman homesteader in Sherman County. ELIZABETH FULTON was born in 1843 and died in 1915. She married Louis Scholl, the architect of Fort Dalles, Fort Simcoe, and Fort Walla Walla. All of these pioneers are buried in the Wasco Sunrise Cemetery.

JESSE EATON was born on March 21, 1826. He died on June 13, 1902. His wife was **MARY ELIZA-BETH BURDEN** who was born on January 8, 1836 in Illinois and died on August 4, 1914. She came to Polk County in 1845. The Eatons were some of the earliest settlers in Sherman County in 1863. They lived near the Wasco cemeteries. They ran the Spanish Hollow (later Wasco) post office from 1870 to 1880. Travelers and stages stopped at the Eaton place, but they did not operate an official stage station. Although they had 13 children, Jesse and Mary were not very compatible, so when they died, their children buried them in different sections of the Wasco Methodist Cemetery! Jesse has a dark diamond-shaped tombstone. Mary has a large dark tombstone.

S. M. GILMORE and **MARTHA A. GILMORE** were some of the very first pioneers to take the Oregon Trail to Oregon. They came to Oregon in 1843. They eventually settled in Sherman County. Their daughter, Brittana, married John Fulton. Mr. Gilmore was born March 17, 1815 and died November 5, 1893. Martha was born on September 11, 1818 and died February 27, 1909 at an age of 90 years, 5 months, and 16 days. Their graves in the Wasco Methodist Cemetery are enclosed within an iron fence.

DANIEL G. LEONARD lived and died by the gun. He was born about 1812 in Vermont and was in Oregon by 1847. He shot a man on Sauvies Island in 1848. He fled to the gold fields in California where he murdered a prospector. Dan returned to Oregon in 1854. He was at Cascade Locks in 1858 and later in The Dalles. He moved to the John Day River in 1861 where he and Amos Underhill established a ferry. In 1863 they started a toll bridge at what later became known as McDonalds Crossing. At the bridge, Dan operated an inn, sold liquor, and ran a post office. Dan had several wives. His daughter, Frances, married Tip Mobley, a famous early settler at Olex. His last wife was Marie (Mary) Gysin, whom he married in 1875. Dan was shot in the head while in bed during the night of January 4, 1878, but he did not die until January 16, 1878. His wife, Mary, and Nathaniel Lindsay, a telegraph lineman, were accused of the murder. Mary was

tried and found not guilty. Nathaniel was never tried. The murder was never solved. Dan is buried in The Dalles Pioneer Cemetery. His stone has been broken and lies on the ground.

ELIZABETH STUART (or **STEWART**) was born on August 31, 1804. She married Peter De Moss, and they had five children. Later she married J. Funkhouser. Her claim to fame is that she was the mother of James M. De Moss, who formed the world famous Lyric Bards. She died September 7, 1893 and is buried in the De Moss Cemetery near Moro.

JAMES M. DE MOSS was born May 15, 1837 in Greensboro, Indiana. He was in Iowa by 1860. He was a minister. In 1862 he came to eastern Oregon. Some historians claim he came to Cove and operated a sawmill. Others say he came to North Powder where he may have been the first settler and where he ran a stage station. The authors have not solved the mystery how James could be in both Cove and North Powder in 1862. He married Elizabeth Bonebroke and they raised a very musical family. In 1872 the family started singing and going on concert tours. They called their group the Lyric Bards. They toured all over the United States, Canada, and Europe. They performed at the Chicago World's Fair in 1893, at the St. Louis Exposition, and at the Lewis and Clark Fair in Portland. They used a Concord stage on part of their tours. In 1883 or earlier, they camped at De Moss Spring north of Moro. They liked the area so much that they bought 800 acres and laid out a town with streets named for poets and composers. They used the town of De Moss Spring as their headquarters between tours. Elizabeth died in 1886 in Roseburg. James died at De Moss Spring on January 17, 1912. A large horizontal cylinder marks his grave in the De Moss Cemetery.

GEORGE GRANT DE MOSS was a son of James M. De Moss. He was born in 1866 in Union County. His wife was **MAMIE AUREL DAVIS,** who was born in 1878 and died in 1952. George was the program manager for the Lyric Bards. He sang and played the cello and cornet. He died in 1933. George and his wife are in the De Moss Cemetery.

Chapter 7

Gilliam County Pioneers

Lonerock was one of the first areas to be settled in Gilliam County. **GEORGE W. BOONE** and his wife **WEALTHY J. BOONE** came to Lonerock in 1871. They came from Pennsylvania to California in 1852. They moved to Salem before coming to Lonerock. The Boones were the first family in the area. George was born in 1821 and died in 1917. Wealthy was born in 1833 and died in 1910. They are buried in the Condon IOOF Cemetery.

JOHN MADDEN came to the Lonerock area about the same time as the George Boones in 1871. He married the Boone's daughter, Madora (Medora). John's tombstone states that he was born in 1840, but the *History of Gilliam County* says he was born on June 13, 1839 in Ireland. He moved to California before coming to Oregon. The Madden's son, George, was the first child born at Lonerock in 1872. They had other children, including John Jr. and Alma. The Maddens ran a store in Lonerock. They, and the Boones, also raised horses and then sheep. John Madden died in 1914 and is buried by the Boones in the Condon Cemetery.

ALBERT HENSHAW was born in Cleveland, Ohio on January 13, 1836. He died in Boise, Idaho on April 10, 1910. His wife was **ISABELLA HENSHAW**, who was born on September 13, 1849. She died on January 24, 1901. The Henshaws are buried in the Condon Cemetery. Albert Henshaw and R. G. Robinson platted Lonerock in October, 1882.

REBECCA ELIZABETH (CARL) PARMAN is said to be the first person buried in the Condon IOOF Cemetery. She died on December 16, 1886 as a result of giving birth to twins. Her infant son and daughter are buried with her. Rebecca and her husband, Giles G. Parman, crossed the plains from Kansas in 1883. They homesteaded five miles west

of Condon in 1884. Rebecca was born on March 16, 1853.

HANS NICHOLI (NICK) ANDERSON was born in Denmark on April 7, 1859. He came to the United States at the age of 17 and settled in Nevada. He married **INGER MARIE (MARY) JACOBSEN** in 1881. They moved to the Condon area in 1883 and homesteaded at Pine Ridge. Mary was born on May 24, 1863 and died on April 12, 1956. Nick died on December 1, 1927. They are buried in the Condon Cemetery.

SILAS ADELBERT RICE was born in October 1837. He married **MARY JANE COTTRELL** in 1865 in Utah. She was born on September 1, 1846. The Rices moved to Idaho and then to Milton, Oregon. In 1884 they moved to two miles north of Condon. They were one of the first homesteaders in the area. Their log cabin is now preserved at the Gilliam County Historical Museum in Condon. Silas died on July 28, 1886 and Mary on May 28, 1924. They are buried in the Condon Cemetery.

GEORGE ALLISON COFFIN was born in 1836. His wife was **ALICE ELIZABETH (SHORB) COFFIN**, who also was born in 1836. They homesteaded on Thirtymile Creek. Previously, they ran a tavern. The Coffins are buried in the Condon Cemetery beside her sister, **MAGGIE K. BROWN** (1855-1945) and Maggie's husband **WILLIAM N. BROWN** (1852-1912).

CLEMENS (CLEM) AUGUSTUS DANNEMAN was born on November 3, 1834 in Germany. He came to the United States in 1856 and on to Oregon in 1879. His wife, **SARAH E. DANNEMAN**, was born on March 7, 1859. Clem was a Civil War veteran. The Dannemans operated a ranch, a stage station where horses were changed, and an inn at Clem. Clem was located north of Condon. Starting in 1884, they also operated the Clem post office. The site of the original Clem was about three miles southeast of the present railroad station of Clem. Some ruins of the old stage station can be seen along Pennington Road. Clem was a member of the State Legislature at one time. Clem died on December 25, 1909, and Sarah died on October 7, 1910. Their graves are marked by rock slabs at the base of the giant Danneman monument in the Condon Cemetery.

LINUS WILSON DARLING was born January 24, 1855. He married **ALCY DELILAH NEAL** at Salem in 1878. They came to Lonerock area in 1878. They owned land near the head of Darling Canyon, which is named for them. Linus built one of the first buildings in Condon in 1887 and ran a drug store there. He also was postmaster for a while. The Darlings are the grandparents of Linus Carl Pauling, who is one of the world's greatest chemists. Pauling won the Nobel Prize in Chemistry and later the Nobel Peace Prize! Delilah Darling died on August 11, 1888 and is buried in the Condon Cemetery with her daughter, Florence, who lived less than two years. Linus Darling died April 15, 1910 and is buried near his wife. Linus has a six foot tombstone with a ball on top.

DAVID B. TRIMBLE was born on November 29, 1841. His wife, **ELIZA Z. TRIMBLE**, was born on December 1, 1850. They were early settlers at Condon. David wanted a post office there, so he named the place Condon after Harry C. Condon, a lawyer in Arlington. David died on January 18, 1922, and Eliza died on August 16, 1920. They are in the Condon Cemetery.

PINKSTON DYER was born in North Carolina on October 5, 1842. He moved to Missouri where he fought in the Civil War. He married **MARY WILOUGHBY** in 1863. She was born in 1840. They came to Clackamas County in 1873 and then onto Silverton. They moved to Ferry Canyon in 1899 to be near their son, James. In 1909 the Dyers retired to Condon. Mary died in 1922, and Pinkston died in 1936. He was Gilliam County's last Civil War veteran. They are in the Condon Cemetery.

ALEXANDER McLAREN HARDIE was born in Scotland on July 19, 1856. He came to Silverton, Oregon by way of Panama in 1874. He moved east

of the Cascade Mountains in 1875 and herded sheep. He moved to Lonerock in 1877 and then homesteaded in the Papersack area west of Lonerock in 1880. His wife, **ELIZABETH ANN PHILLIPS**, was from Lonerock when he married her in 1881. Alex's father, **ALEXANDER DICK HARDIE**, left Scotland to join his son in 1881. His wife **ANN McLAREN HARDIE,** and other children joined them in 1882. The elder Hardie was born on October 18, 1834 and died on September 23, 1909. Ann was born on November 2, 1834 and died on September 30, 1918. Their son, Alex, died on December 10, 1927. All of the Hardies are now buried in the Condon Cemetery.

CHARLES JAMES QUINN was born on October 20, 1847. He moved from Canada to California in 1880. He married **CATHERINE (KATE) JANE GIBBONS**, who was born February 2, 1849. They moved to near Arlington in 1883. He built many of the buildings in Condon, Fossil, and Mayville. He also was a justice of the peace. Catherine died October 21, 1912 and Charles on March 11, 1917. They share an eight foot white obelisk in Condon's St. Joseph Cemetery.

HENRY WILKINS was born on January 16, 1867 in Iowa. He married **CARRIE ANN CRUM** in 1891. She was born January 12, 1873 at Summerville. The Wilkins were early settlers in the Clem area. Carrie died February 18, 1922 and Henry on May 15, 1938. They are buried in the Condon Cemetery.

ELIJAH W. RHEA was born on February 27, 1824 and died on April 7, 1883. He built the first building in Arlington (then called Alkali) in 1880. He built a hotel there in 1882. He was the postmaster of Alkali. Elijah died from too much opium in an attempt to sober up from being drunk. He is buried in the Arlington Cemetery.

Rock Creek and the town of Olex area were the first settled area in Gilliam County. Olex was settled even before Lonerock and was an important trade center by the late 1860's. Olex was named after Alex Smith, the first to settle in the area by 1865.

CONRAD SCHOTT was born in 1832 in Germany. He moved to St. Louis, and at 21 years of age traveled to California. He moved again to Corvallis where he married **MARY FRANCIS MOBLEY** in 1865. She was the daughter of William Mobley, and she was born in 1847. They came to Olex in 1867 (some say 1865), the second family there. In 1875 they built the first store and the first school on their ranch. They had ten children. Three of their daughters died at an early age: **GRACIE AENA** (1878-1892), **LIZZIE A.** died November 4, 1872 at four years, and **ELLA G.** died November 25, 1872 at one year. Conrad died in 1903 and his wife in 1930. All are buried in the Olex Cemetery.

THOMAS (TIP) C. MOBLEY was born in 1852 in either Kentucky or Missouri. His family moved to California in 1855 and then to Corvallis in 1863. Tip drove cattle to the Idaho mines in 1869. In 1872 he moved to Olex to be near his sister, Mrs. Conrad Schott. He spent the first year about five miles up Rock Creek from Olex. Then, he moved to Alex Smith's place about a mile down stream from Olex. Smith apparently wanted to leave the area and gave his land to Tip. Tip married **FRANCES LEONARD** in 1876. She was born at Cascade Locks in 1858, the daughter of Daniel Leonard, who for many years operated a ferry and then a bridge across the John Day River on the Oregon Trail. Daniel was murdered by a gunshot to the head. The murder was never really solved, but his wife was acquitted of the murder. Tip was mostly a cattleman but also raised some wheat. He was a true cowboy who made his lariats from horse hair. He was well liked by his neighbors and by the many Indians who traveled through or stopped to trade. The Mobley's learned the Chinook jargon in order to converse with the Indians. Tip and Frances adopted a baby, Lulu Hockett, whose mother died in childbirth in 1895. Lulu married George Irby. The Irby family still lives on the old Mobley Ranch. Tip died in 1928 and Francis in 1940. They are buried in the Olex Cemetery.

In his later life, Tip's father, **WILLIAM MOBLEY** moved to Olex to live with his son. William was born on March 20, 1819 in Kentucky, and died on June 23, 1893. He had married Caroline Klinger, who was born in 1828 and who died in California in childbirth. William died June 23, 1893 and is in the Olex Cemetery.

JOSEPH SMITH was born on December 22, 1804 in Brookville, Maine. He died May 12, 1884 and is in the Olex Cemetery. We have no more information about him, but he was the earliest born interned there.

WILLIAM GEORGE FLETT was born on September 25, 1842 in Washington County, Oregon. He was a saddle maker in Portland for a while and then worked for the Hudson's Bay Company for a year. He ran a packtrain from The Dalles to Canyon City and then to Boise. In 1870 he moved to Rock Creek eight miles south of Olex and about two miles north of Wolf Hollow. He raised cattle and farmed on three sections of land. In 1872 he went to the Willamette Valley to marry **LYDIA DOUGHTY** of Yamhill County. She was born on December 23, 1853. Her mother was an Indian. Her father was an American Fur Company trapper. He once was a partner of Joe Meek and was important in the formation of Oregon's Provisional Government. He was one of the writers of the government at Champoeg, and his name is on the monument there. Mr. Flett established the post office of Flettville in 1881. He also had the Flett School on his ranch. William died in 1923 and Lydia in 1903. Three of the Flett children died at an early age of tuberculosis. One daughter, **FANNIE GERRISH**, lived from 1881 to 1933. The Fletts are buried in the Flett Cemetery on their ranch in a fenced enclosure about 200 yards west of the gravel road along Rock Creek. An eight foot monument carries the name of the parents and the following children: **REUBEN R. FLETT** (1873-1921), **ELDA P. FLETT** (1886-1908) and **DOTTIE FLETT** (1888-1905). In the same cemetery there also are 10 small stones marked "Unknown."

For many years the main store in Olex was the Wade Store operated by several Wades. It had a dance hall on the second floor. The mother of the Wade children who ran the store was **MARTHA ANN (STEPHENSON GARLETT) WADE**. She was a widow with five children who married William Nash Wade about 1863. Martha died on August 19, 1900 from typhoid fever. She was 68 years old and is buried in the Olex Cemetery in a fenced enclosure with other Wades.

JOHN CHARLES COONEY was born on June 14, 1846 in Ireland. He came to the United States as a stone mason. He married **MARY ELLEN SUMMERS** in Iowa. She was born in 1857. He built stone bridges for the Santa Fe Railroad to California. They moved to Salt Lake, and then in 1883 they settled on Matney Flat near Condon. John built many of the original stone buildings in Condon. He also ran sheep and a homestead on Snipton in 1890. He operated a freight outfit between Arlington and Condon. John died October 4, 1919 and Mary in 1931. They are in the St. Joseph Cemetery in Condon.

JAMES PULLIAM CASON was born on January 5, 1832 in Missouri. His mother was a sister of Ben Holliday, the stage coach "king." James and his parents came to Gladstone, Oregon in 1843. He married **MARY E. MARSH** in 1853. Mary was born October 8, 1836 in Illinois. The Marsh family started across the plains in 1847. The mother, Louisa (Meeker) Marsh, died on the Oregon Trail in Idaho. The family stopped at the Whitman Mission where the father, Walter Marsh, was killed in the Whitman Massacre. Mary Marsh was captured by the Indians until Peter Skene Ogden obtained her release. She then lived with the A. J. Lovejoy family in Portland. Mr. Lovejoy wanted to name the place Boston, but by the toss of a coin, it became the town of Portland. James and Mary moved in 1868 to Rhea Creek near Ruggs in Morrow County. Cason Canyon is named for them. They moved to Ione in 1878 and then to Shutler Flat south of Arlington in 1882 where they raised wheat. The Casons had ten children. James died on September 6, 1887 and is buried in the Arlington Cemetery. Mary and family moved to the Kahler Basin. She died on April 6, 1907 and is buried in the Haystack Cemetery north of Spray.

EDMUND ALPHONSO STINCHFIELD was born October 10, 1858 in Maine. He came to near Heppner in 1867 and later moved to Mayville and raised sheep. He married a widow, **PHOEBE (PHEBE) McCONNELL** in 1887. Phoebe and her previous husband had platted the town of Clyde in 1884. They named it after the first blacksmith in the area. The name was soon changed to Mayville. The Stinchfields bought for taxes the first log cabin at Mayville. This cabin had been built by E. A. Evans. Later, the Stinchfields built a large two-story house in Mayville. This home is now in a state of disrepair. Edmund died in 1935 and Phoebe in 1938. They are buried in the Mayville Cemetery.

WILLIAM P. WEST was born February 24, 1842 in Denmark (His tombstone lists the date as 1841.) He came to New York in 1859 and then on to St. Louis. He traveled to California and mined until 1861 when he went to the Idaho mines. In 1863 he settled on Rock Creek nine miles west of Olex to farm and raise stock. He was one of the first settlers in Gilliam County. He married **MARY L. MULKEY** in 1876 on Rock Creek. She was born in Josephine County on March 6, 1860. William died in 1931 and Mary in 1920. They are buried in the Arlington Cemetery.

JEREMIAH A. CRUM was born in Pennsylvania on February 14, 1846. He worked in a flour mill in Philadelphia for a while before moving to Illinois at eighteen. In 1861 he moved to Virginia City, Montana where he ran the first flour mill in that territory. He moved to Walla Walla in 1867 or 1868 and went to the mines. He moved to Summerville and ran a flour mill for his wife's brother, J. H. Rinehart, for five years. He moved to Clackamas County and farmed until 1883 when he settled at Olex. He built a flour mill at Olex in 1885—the first mill between The Dalles and Pendleton. He married **SARAH E. RINEHART** in 1871. She was born March 6, 1853 in Iowa. Her father was the famous pioneer, **LEWIS B. RINEHART**, who was born September 5, 1801 and who died in Summerville in 1882. They crossed the plains to near Eugene in 1854. She moved to Summerville when she was 17. A tragedy struck the family in September 1898 when three children died of typhoid fever, and the father died a few days later on October 8, 1898 of the same disease. The children were **WILLARD F. R. CRUM** who died September 8, 1898 aged 22 years, 10 days; **EUGENE J. CRUM** died September 16, 1898 aged 19 years, 11 months, 23 days; and **FRANKLIN H. CRUM** died September 13, 1898 aged 16 years and 3 days. Jeremiah and his three sons are in the Arlington Cemetery under a long concrete slab with four small sloping-faced tombstones on top. Sarah died in 1932 and is buried nearby.

Chapter 8
Wheeler County Pioneers

CHRISTIAN W. MEYER was born in 1819 in Germany. He was in the California gold rush of 1849. He and partner, "Alkali" Frank Huat (Hewatt), were the first settlers in the entire area around Mitchell. In 1863 they settled along Meyers Canyon by the road between The Dalles and Canyon City. Their place was five miles northwest of the present Mitchell. They operated a stage station and inn and raised a fine garden and orchard as well as a wheat field. Meyer married Meta, who was half Indian. Alkali Frank moved to Eightmile Creek near The Dalles. Meyer died on February 9, 1903 and is buried in the old Mitchell Cemetery east of town.

HENRY H. WHEELER was born September 7, 1826 in Pennsylvania. He crossed the plains to California in 1857. In 1863 he came to The Dalles and the next year started a stage line between The Dalles and the gold-mining town of Canyon City. In addition to passengers, his stage carried mail and gold. On September 7, 1866, Indians attacked Wheeler's stage about three miles northeast of Mitchell. He was shot through both cheeks, but he and H. C. Page were able to escape. They used two of the stage horses to get to Meyers Station a few miles to the northwest. In 1872 Wheeler started operating the famous Corncob Ranch near Spray. He opened a post office there in 1877. He left the Corncob Ranch in 1878 and homesteaded on Girds Creek. Henry married DORCAS L. MONROE in 1875. She was born on October 18, 1848. The Wheelers moved to Mitchell in 1904. Dorcas died on March 8, 1911 and Henry on March 26, 1916. They have tombstones beside a large Wheeler monument in Mitchell's IOOF or West Cemetery.

EZEKIEL H. WATERMAN was born on February 24, 1812 in New York. He married Mary A. Straud. They moved to Missouri in 1840 and then took a wagon train to California in 1852. They moved to near Salem in 1858. Ezekiel and son, John W. Waterman took squatter's rights on Waterman Flat northeast of Mitchell in 1862. Mary had died in Marion County in 1866, and Ezekiel married NANCY M. SMITH, who was born March 10, 1837. After several years, Ezekiel sold out to John Fopiano and moved to The Dalles. He ran a loan office business and did well. Ezekiel died December 28, 1902 and Nancy on March 6, 1913. They have tombstones beside a Waterman monument in The Dalles IOOF Cemetery.

JAMES WASHINGTON CHAMBERS was born on September 6, 1817 at the Hermitage in Tennessee. He was the nephew of Andrew Jackson on his mother's side of the family. He came to Oregon in the 1830's as a mountain man. He returned to St. Louis and married the widow Scoggin, who had five children. James led a wagon train to Oregon in 1844. They stopped at The Dalles where daughter Mary Jane Chambers was born in 1845. He built a flat boat to go down the Columbia River and settled near Hillsboro. In 1868 and '69, James scouted the Fossil area for a new home. In 1870 he and other members of his family, the Hoovers and Woodson Scoggin, came to Hoover Creek near the present town of Fossil. They were the first settlers in the Fossil area. James' wife visited the ranch a short time and returned to the Tualatin Valley. He raised horses and cattle. James was thrown from a horse and broke his neck. He died July 11, 1877. He is buried above the ranch on Hoover Creek. His tombstone is surrounded by tall sagebrush.

THOMAS BENTON HOOVER was born August 16, 1839. In 1844 he traveled the Oregon Trail to six miles north of Hillsboro with his parents. In 1864 he married MARY JANE CHAMBERS, who was born on December 22, 1845 at The Dalles. She was the daughter of James Washington Chambers. They moved to Hoover Creek north of Fossil in 1870. In 1876, Thomas established a post office at his ranch. He and Thomas Watson started a store in 1881 at what became the town of Fossil. The Hoovers also built a home in Fossil that is still used. Thomas died on January 19, 1896 and Mary Jane on September 29, 1934. They have small tombstones inside an enclosure with a tall Hoover monument in the Fossil IOOF Cemetery.

THOMAS WATSON was born on December 29, 1828. He was Thomas Benton Hoover's partner in the first store in Fossil. He died August 11, 1900 and is in the Fossil IOOF Cemetery.

GEORGE JACKSON METTEER was born on October 31, 1837 in Pennsylvania. His family was in the Oatman party, which was attacked by Indians. The Metteers escaped and reached California in 1851. George mined in California and Idaho. He arrived in Marion County in 1858. He married **MARY ANN SMITH** in 1862. She was born on October 3, 1843 (the date is 1844 on her tombstone) in Iowa. The Metteers moved to Pine Creek west of Fossil and near Clarno in 1873. They were the first homesteaders in that area. George built the first sawmill in Wheeler County. They ran a ferry across the John Day River near Clarno. He had a brick kiln near Fossil and made the bricks for the Fossil Courthouse, a Fossil grade school, and a bank. George died on December 6, 1916 or 1917 and Mary on November 24, 1919. They are buried under a large disintegrating concrete slab in the Fossil IOOF Cemetery.

THOMAS MAJOR ANDREW JACKSON PARRISH was born in 1830. In the 1840's he moved from Texas to Oregon. He married **ELEANOR BEERS** in 1870. She was the grand daughter of Alason Beers a provisional governor of Oregon. Andrew moved to the Waldron area in 1870. Parrish Creek is named for them. Apparently, after 1871 they lived near the mouth of Parrish Creek across the John Day River from Spray. Andrew died on April 1, 1894 at an age of 64 years, 2 months, and 22 days. The Parrishs are buried in the Richmond Cemetery. There is an iron monument

with "Father" and "Mother" tombstones at its side. No dates are on Eleanor's stone.

ROBERT H. DEDMAN was born in Tennessee on June 26, 1847. He came to the John Day River area near Twickenham in 1867 or '68. He probably was the first settler in that area. He married **SARAH J. WILLIAMS** in 1877. She was born on September 10, 1850 in Illinois. He built a log fort house as protection from raiding Indians. The squared logs were ten inches thick. Augered holes along the sides were for rifles. In 1885 the Dedmans moved to near Waldron, then to Richmond. In 1912 they moved to Mitchell. Robert died in 1924 and Sarah in 1934. They are in the Richmond Cemetery.

RODERICK N. DONNELLY was born in 1855 in Tennessee. He came to Richmond in the 1870's and raised sheep. He married **REBECCA JANE KEYES**. She also was born in 1855. Roderick was elected to the State Legislature and introduced the law to form Wheeler County in 1899. He donated the land where the town of Richmond was established. Today, Richmond is one of the most interesting ghost towns in Oregon. Roderick died in 1936 and Jane in 1938. They are buried in the Fossil IOOF Cemetery.

DAVID HAMILTON was born February 27, 1830 in New York. He came to Douglas County in 1855. He married **MARY BYARS** in 1858. She was born October 3, 1842 and came to Oregon from Iowa in 1853. They moved to Cottonwood Creek three miles south of Fossil in 1870 or '71, the third family in the Fossil area. Their son, Myron, was murdered in Condon on September 6, 1894 by James Barnard, who committed suicide the next day. David and Mary are buried in the Fossil Masonic Cemetery under a disintegrating concrete slab. Most of the inscriptions can no longer be read.

ISAAC N. SARGENT was born in 1817 in Chester, Vermont. He was teaching school in Wisconsin by 1838. He crossed the plains to Oregon in 1862 to farm on Fivemile Creek near The Dalles. He freighted to the mines at Canyon City. He moved to Mitchell in 1867 and was one of the first settlers there. He platted the town of Mitchell in 1885. Later, the Sargents moved to The Dalles. Isaac had married **HANNA H. BROWN** in 1838. She was born in Springfield, Vermont on July 14, 1817. Hanna died on December 8, 1904 and Isaac in 1907. They are buried in a large concrete structure in The Dalles IOOF Cemetery.

W. W. (BRAWDIE OR BROADY) JOHNSON was born on May 20, 1847. He started the town of Mitchell when in April 1873 he set up a blacksmith shop at the site and established a post office. In 1876 he was the blacksmith on the Malheur Indian Reservation in Harney County. He was the first postmaster at the town of Harney. After Fort Harney was abandoned, he moved to Silver Creek to ranch. In 1879, he moved to Burns and ran a hotel and a saloon. He was elected a US deputy marshall of Harney County. His wife was **CAROLINE JOHNSON**, who was born on January 13, 1849. Mr. Johnson died May 12, 1906, and Caroline died on April 17, 1929. They are buried in the Burns Cemetery.

HANNAH MORGAN WARD was born in 1822 and died in 1901. She came to Oregon over the Oregon Trail in 1847 with an Iowa party.

Chapter 9

Grant County Pioneers

WILLIAM C. (or A.) ALLRED is generally credited as being the first person to discover gold at Canyon City on June 8, 1862. He was a member of a party of gold seekers from California when they made the strike. However, they continued on for a few days before returning to Canyon Creek. Upon their return they found the creek lined with miners. The Allred party established the rich Prairie Diggings a few miles to the east. Each of their claims yielded $10,000 and worth $20 a pan in the days when gold was worth $20.70 an ounce! We know nothing more about him except that he died in 1906 and is buried in the Canyon City Cemetery.

GEORGE I. HAZELTINE was born in 1836. He was one of the first to reach the mines at Canyon City in 1862 from the California mines. His mining claim was in the middle of what is now the town of John Day. He established the first flour mill at John Day. He also became a famous photographer. His wife was EMELINE C. HAZELTINE, who was born in 1843. Mr. Hazeltine died in 1918 and Emeline in 1936. They have a large monument in the Canyon City Cemetery.

NEAL (NEIL) McNULTY was one of the first to mine at Prairie Diggings east of Canyon City. Later he operated a saloon. He died November 6, 1876 and is buried in the Canyon City St. Andrews Cemetery.

BRADFORD C. TROWBRIDGE was born in 1836 in New York. Ten years later he was in Illinois. He travelled to Yreka, California to mine in 1859. In 1862 he came to Canyon City following the search for gold, but he soon filed on the first homestead in Grant County. His farm was across the river from John Day. He raised vegetables and fruit for the miners. He also raised several famous race horses. He married MARJORY MILLINEY in 1888. She was

born in 1850. Marjory died in 1923 and Bradford in 1836. They are buried in the Canyon City Cemetery.

CHARLES BELSHAW was born on March 9, 1833 in England. He came to Indiana with his parents in 1834. The family moved to Eugene in 1853. Charles went to California in search of gold and then he came to Canyon City in 1862. In 1864 he started farming and fruit raising about 22 miles west of the town of John Day. He originated the Belshaw prune. He also taught music. He married JANE LUCE in 1859. She was born March 20, 1839 and died July 25, 1913. The Belshaws are buried in the Canyon City Cemetery.

JOHN HERBURGER was born in Germany on February 15, 1805. In the early 1860's he began farming along the John Day River in the vicinity of Mount Vernon. He sold potatoes to the miners at Canyon City for twenty five cents a pound. His wife was MRS. G. (or C.) METSCHAN who was born June 23, 1811. John died September 14, 1878 and his wife on February 20, 1886. They are buried in the Canyon City Cemetery.

DAVID W. JENKINS was born August 22, 1811 in Scotland. The family moved to New York in 1832. David worked in the Brooklyn Navy Yards until 1844 when he moved to Texas and then to California in 1848. In California he was a boat builder. He established the town of Arcadia, California. In 1863 he started packing to the mines in Grant County, and the next year he homesteaded seven and a half miles west of John Day. David had a famous black stallion named Mount Vernon. He built a stone house with rifle ports to protect the horse from thieves and Indians. The stone building still stands just north of US 26 about a mile and a half east of the town of Mount Vernon. Legend says that the Indians kept stealing the horse to breed their mares. The Indians always returned the stallion but David was never pleased. During the Bannock War of 1878, neighbors took shelter in the stone house. David married **ANNIE (ANNA) M. RILEY** in 1861. She was born March 15, 1835. David died April 11, 1904 and Annie on December 21, 1908. They share a tall monument in the Canyon City Cemetery.

JOSEPH CAYTON OLIVER was born on March 16, 1850 in the Azore Islands. He came to the United States as a stowaway when he was 16. He crossed the Isthmus of Panama and made his way to Portland in 1866. He came to Canyon City and worked in the mines until 1878. He worked on a farm for the August Gregg family. After August died, Joe married Mrs. Gregg. She was **MARY ELIZABETH (LIZZIE) GREGG**, born in 1848. In 1880 the Olivers moved to their ranch east of John Day. They raised cattle and supplied the John Day area with milk. Eventually the Oliver Ranch had over 54,000 acres, 4,500 cattle and 7,000 sheep. The Oliver sons became very prominent citizens in the John Day region. Joe died in 1921 and Lizzie in 1926. They are buried in the Canyon City Cemetery.

PETER KUHL was born in Germany in 1847. In 1867 he came to Iowa, and in 1868 he crossed the plains to the coast and then to Canyon City in 1870. He established a shop and feed store. He started a ranch on Indian Creek about 12 miles east of Canyon City. He married **JULIA L. SELS** in 1878. The Kuhl Ranch is still in the family. Peter died in 1907 and Julia in 1920. They are buried in the Canyon City Cemetery.

IKE GUKER was born in 1860. He was not one of the early gold miners in the Canyon City area but in 1897, he discovered one of the richest gold pockets ever found in the area. His mine was east of Canyon City and north of Canyon Mountain. He took $50,000 to $65,000 from a hole the size of a house! His discovery started a second gold rush to the John Day region. Ike died in 1947 and is buried in the Canyon City Cemetery.

ALFRED HYDE was born on September 6, 1810. His wife was **MARGARET HYDE**. The Hyde's settled seven miles east of Prairie City in 1871 and raised vegetables and grain. Their son Heil was

born in New York in 1841. Heil fought in the Civil war in Co. E, 98 N.Y. Volunteer Infantry. Alfred died on August 11, 1893. Margaret died in 1887. They are buried in the Prairie City Cemetery.

H. H. HYDE was born in New York September 24, 1812. Apparently, he was the brother of Alfred Hyde. His wife was **SUSAN HYDE**, who was born in Kentucky on September 22, 1817. H. H. Hyde established the first store in Prairie City. He died July 8, 1881 and Susan on December 25, 1888. They are buried in the Prairie City Cemetery.

FRANK FLAGEOLLET (FLAGEOLETTE) was born in France about 1820. He built the first hotel and the first saloon in Prairie City. He died December 17, 1888 and is buried in the Prairie City Cemetery.

MARSHALL S. KEENEY was born October 1, 1850 in Missouri. He came to California with his parents in 1857. They moved to Linn County in 1858 and then to Eugene. In 1865 or 1861 he moved to Umatilla with his parents. He drove the family's band of sheep. He went to California again for a short time and then back to Birch Creek in Umatilla County. He drove cattle to Idaho and then went to Wallowa County in 1873. Marshall again travelled to California before moving to Long Creek to operate a store with brother, Thomas in 1874. He married **CARRIE CONGER** of Long Creek in 1882. She died October 27, 1889, aged 28 years, 8 months, and 6 days. Marshall died in 1918. They are buried in the Long Creek Cemetery.

THOMAS B. KEENEY, brother of Marshall Keeney, was born September 10, 1852 in Missouri. After considerable moving around, he came to Umatilla County with his parents and raised sheep. He operated a store with Marshall in Long Creek. He married **NANCY ELLEN SNODDERLY** of Prineville in 1882. She was born on June 13, 1857 and died October 8, 1899. Thomas died in 1923. Both are buried in the Long Creek Cemetery.

JOSEPH W. KEENEY was an older brother of Marshall and Thomas. He was born in 1849 and died in 1921. He started a store in Long Creek about 1879. Joe is buried in the Long Creek Cemetery.

CHARLES BALLANCE was born in Illinois on either November 5 or December 5, 1840. He moved

Pioneers Born Before 1800

Peter Zell Sr.

Joe Nicols Sr.

Levi Scott

Joseph Lavadour

Robert T. Baldwin

Nancy Price

Nancy Stone

Pioneeers
of the
Bannock War

John Vey

James R. Daulby

James Myers

Charles Jewell

Aldrich

Harrison Hale

Pioneers of The Dalles Area and Wasco County

Wallace

Ezekiel and Nancy M. Waterman

Hampton Kelly

Joseph and Lucinda Haynes

Joseph and Jane Sherar

Snipes

Rev. Ezra Fisher

Elizabeth Smailes

W. L. and Hanna Ward

Humason

James M. Grater

Phoebe McAtte

Nathan Olney

Zylpha Henderson

Dan Leonard

Fredrick Homer Balch

Omar Pratt

Howard Maupin

William Heisler house

Sherman County Pioneers

James Fulton

John and Brittana Fulton

Samuel and Palmira Price

Samuel Price

James M. DeMoss

Jesse Eaton

Gilliam County Pioneers

Martha Gilmore

Louis Scholl

William Mobley

Conrad Schott

Thomas (Tip) Mobley

Frances Mobley

Linus Darling

Rebecca Parmin

W. H. Pentecost

W. G. Flett

William Carroll Cecil

Wheeler County Pioneers

Thomas M.A.J. Parrish

Hannah Morgan Ward

James Chamber

Thomas B. Hoover

Stephen Carroll

Christian W. Meyer

H. H. Wheeler and Dorcas Wheeler

Grant County Pioneers

Charles and Jane Belshaw

Trowbridge

D. W. Jenkins

H. H. Hyde

Richard Mascall

Enoch Conger

Neal McNulty

to Iowa and then Kansas. In 1860 he travelled to the Pikes Peak mines. During the Civil War, he was in both the Kansas Infantry and the Kansas Cavalry where he became a first lieutenant. He married **ELIZABETH J. RICKER** in 1862. They moved to San Francisco in 1874, then to Linn County, and finally to one mile east of Long Creek. Elizabeth was born in 1840 and died in 1877. Charles died on July 4, 1911. They are buried in the Long Creek Cemetery.

ENOCH CONGER and PERMELIA (PAMELIA on tombstone) **CONGER** were early settlers in the Long Creek area in 1881. Enoch was born July 29, 1819 and Pamelia on April 11, 1826. He died August 6, 1894 and she on January 15, 1915. They are buried in the Long Creek Cemetery.

JOHN W. CONGER was born March 7, 1861 in Oregon. He was the son of Enoch and Pamelia Conger. In 1879 he homesteaded six miles north of Long Creek and raised sheep. He married Olive Baird in 1888. He died in 1929 and is buried in the Fox Cemetery.

JAMES M. SHIELDS was born on January 21, 1831 in Georgia. He moved to Arkansas in 1859. In 1863 he joined Company A, 2nd Arkansas Infantry and fought many battles under General Steele. In 1877 he rode a horse across the plains and settled in the Long Creek area where he may have been the first pioneer there. His second marriage was to **SARAH A. McWHORTER** in 1856. They had eleven children. She was born in 1839 and died in 1923. James died March 2, 1903. They are buried in the Long Creek Cemetery.

FRANK McGIRR is claimed to be the first permanent settler in the Fox Valley. He was born January 23, 1860 in California. He took part in a large cattle drive to Wyoming in 1879. He came to Fox Valley in 1880 and raised stock. He married Henrietta Hart in 1880. Frank died November 29, 1909. He has a white seven foot obelisk in the Fox Cemetery.

JAMES MURPHY was born on November 23, 1832. During the Civil War, he was in Company D, 16th Iowa Infantry and was with General Sherman on his march to the sea. His wife was **MARY MURPHY**, who was born November 20, 1838. The

family moved from Iowa to Missouri, Kansas, Texas, and to Walla Walla in 1881. They moved to Fox Valley in 1882. James died October 16, 1897 and Mary on July 11, 1906. They are buried in the Fox Cemetery. James shares a tombstone with **SARAH BUCKMASTER,** who probably was his mother. Sarah was born November 25, 1815 and died June 16, 1883.

JOHN H. HAMILTON was born April 5, 1826 in Kentucky. He moved to Indiana and then to Missouri in 1851. He crossed the plains to near Oregon City in 1852. During the trip three of his sisters died in one night of cholera. In 1848 he married **MARY J. ROBINS,** who was born April 7, 1828. They moved to the future site of Hamilton in 1872, which is named for them. They were the first settlers in the area. Mary died May 4, 1900 and John on December 2, 1909. They are in the Hamilton Cemetery.

WILLIAM NEAL was born April 15, 1815 in Indiana. He married **MAHALA M. PARKER** who also was born in Indiana on May 10 or May 19, 1813. They moved to Illinois and then to Missouri. In 1850 they took the Oregon Trail to Marion County. They moved to the Heppner area in 1868 and then took the first wagon to the monument area where they settled six miles west of the present town of Monument. Their son, **NAPOLEON BONEPARTE NEAL** was born in 1856 and died in 1925. William died July 17, 1908 and Mahala on May 17, 1904. All are buried in the Monument Cemetery.

EMMET (EMMETT on tombstone) **COCHRAN** was born February 6, 1869 near Oregon City. His parents were William W. Cochran and **SARAH M. COCHRAN.** Sarah died August 2, 1908, aged 60 years, 5 months, 6 days. The family moved to west of Monument in 1870. They were among the very earliest settlers of the area. They raised cattle and sheep. Emmet married Emma Allen of Monument in 1889. Her parents were **WILLIAMSON ALLEN** and **MARY CATHERINE ALLEN.** Williamson was born September 26, 1839 and died May 22, 1901. Mary was born in 1845 and died in 1935. Emmet Cochran died in 1944. All are buried in the Monument Cemetery. **AMANDA COCHRAN,** a relative of

Emmet, is buried with them. She was born August 11, 1833 and died May 4, 1900.

The Mascal family was early settlers in the Dayville area. **RICHARD MASCAL** was born on February 25, 1828. His wife was **SOPHIA J. MAS-CAL,** who was born on May 20, 1828. Fossils were found on their ranch, which became headquarters for famous geologists such as Thomas Condon. The Mascal fossil beds are named for the family. Richard died April 16, 1881 and Sophia on April 23, 1883. They are buried in the Dayville Cemetery.

Chapter 10

Morrow County Pioneers

WILLIAM YANCY CECIL was born May 24, 1819 in England. He came to Illinois and then to Missouri. He married Mary Ellen Robertson (or Robinson) in 1847. In 1862, the Cecils crossed the plains on the Oregon Trail. When their wagon broke down on Willow Creek, they decided to settle at what became the hamlet of Cecil. At that time, there was a large spring where other settlers came to get water. The Cecils established a post office there in 1867. William died November 6, 1898 and is buried in the Arlington Cemetery. Two of the Cecil children are buried in an isolated cemetery on a bench west of Willow Creek and east of Highway 74, about two miles south of Heppner Junction. Son, WALTER CECIL died on February 13, 1877, aged 5 years, 7 months, 21 days. Daughter, ANNA LAURA CECIL died February 17, 1877, aged 7 years, 11 months, 15 days. The children died only four days apart, evidently from some epidemic.

COLUMBUS (LUM) A. RHEA was born May 8, 1845 in Missouri. In 1853 he crossed the plains from Missouri to the Willamette Valley at Eugene. In 1864 Lum found a spring on Rhea Creek and settled there. He was the first settler on the creek and built the first house there. In 1868 he married EMALINE SOPHRONIA ADKINS. She had lived in the Willamette Valley. She was born on January 6, 1848. Eventually, Lum owned over 7000 acres and large herds of cattle and sheep. He founded the First National Bank of Heppner. Emaline died on May 12, 1900 and Lum in 1934. They are buried in the Heppner Cemetery.

THOMAS W. AYERS was born on March 28, 1840 in Iowa. He came to Oregon, and in 1862, Tom and his brother, William, came to Butter Creek at what later became the famous Vey Ranch. Tom farmed and raised cattle on the ranch. For four years he also ran a pack train from Umatilla Landing to the mines at Granite. He charged 20 cents a pound for freight and $30 for cattle. By 1878 he had 1180 cattle and 325 horses. In 1883 he sold out to the Vey brothers and moved to Heppner where he started a livery and a harness business. He also ran a real estate office and a loan business. He was treasurer, and later secretary, of the local light and water company. Tom had married SARAH ELLEN BRUCE in Iowa. She died November 6, 1878, aged 38 years, 9 months, and 28 days. In 1881 he married NANCY ELLEN (ELLA) McCLURE. She died November 26, 1887, aged 27 years, 11 months, and 14 days. Tom was married a third time to Mrs. Eliza J. Smith in 1888. Tom died August 28, 1909 and is buried in the Heppner Cemetery with his first two wives.

WILLIAM AYERS was born in Indiana on May 6, 1835. The Ayers moved to Iowa where William's brother, Thomas, was born. William took the Oregon Trail to Oregon City in 1853. He went to the California mines where he made a large sum of money. He returned to Iowa, but in 1862 the Ayers moved to Butter Creek. He acquired additional land on Little Butter Creek in 1870. William also owned land at Salem as well as a home in Heppner. He owned over 6000 sheep. William had married MATILDA C. BOORD in 1857. She was born on November 26, 1836. William died September 10, 1913 and Matilda on June 10, 1916. They are buried in the Heppner Cemetery.

AMANUEL C. PETTEYS was born August 8, 1836 in New York. His parents were Seneca and OLIVE (TOWNER) PETTEYS. They moved to Michigan in 1841 where Seneca died in 1850. Amanuel left for Oregon in 1853 and in 1854, he was in Salem. He mined for awhile. In 1868 he brought cattle to the forks of Rhea and Willow

Creeks three miles east of Ione. He ran the Petteys-ville post office for 14 years. He became county assessor in 1896. He married **CATHERINE (KATIE) GIENGER** in 1877. She was born in 1855, the daughter of **GEORGE GIENGER** and Elizabeth Gienger. Amanuel's mother was living with him. She was born in 1815 and died in 1884. George Gienger died on November 26, 1883, aged 62 years. Amanuel died June 18, 1919 and Katie in 1931. All are buried in the Petteys Cemetery on the plateau not far from Ione.

ORIN EDWARD FARNSWORTH was born on November 27, 1846 in New Hampshire. During the Civil War, he was in Company K, 7th Kansas Cavalry. He came to California by way of the isthmus of Panama in 1865. He arrived in Portland in 1869. In 1873 he married **CATHERINE (KATIE) PRAY.** She was born in 1850. They moved to Ruggs in 1874 to raise sheep. Orin died May 14, 1919 and Katie in 1929. They are buried in the Heppner Cemetery.

EDWARD CLUFF was born in November 1829 in Ireland. He came to Indiana and then to Missouri in 1849. He went on to Yamhill County in 1850 and then to the mines in California. He returned to Oregon and participated in the Indian War of 1855-56. He moved to Morrow County in 1870 and on to the site of Ione in 1872. He was the first settler near Ione. Later he was the justice of peace. He raised cattle and alfalfa. He died on March 31, 1906. He has a nine foot obelisk in the Ione Cemetery.

WILLIAM PENLAND was the founder of the town of Lexington. He brought sheep to the town in 1868. These were the first sheep in Morrow County. Penland became known as the "sheep king of Morrow County." Lexington was platted on his claim in 1885. The town was named by his wife **JANE PENLAND** after her birth place, Lexington, Kentucky. She was born in 1843, and died on October 22, 1917. William was born in 1839 and died February 25, 1901. They are buried in the Lexington Penland Cemetery.

JACKSON L. MORROW was born October 18, 1827 in Kentucky. Jackson went to Iowa where he married **NANCY McQUEEN**. She was born on July 22, 1829 in Indiana. In 1853 they crossed the plains to near Olympia, Washington and set up a mercantile business. He is credited as the founder of Tumwater, Washington. Jackson was a Lt. Colonel in the Indian War of 1855-56. He moved to La Grande in 1863 and operated a store. He was elected treasurer of Union County. Jackson moved to Heppner and established a mercantile business with Henry Heppner for whom the town of Heppner is named. Jackson Morrow became a state legislator in 1885 and organized Morrow County, which is named for him. Nancy Morrow died November 22, 1882, and she has a 12 foot monument in the Morrow plot which is enclosed inside an iron fence in the Heppner Cemetery. Jackson died on September 22, 1899 and is in the Heppner Cemetery also.

THOMAS MORGAN was born July 9, 1842 in Illinois. His parents moved to Benton County when he was four. While still a boy, he carried mail from Corvallis to Oakland. He went to the Idaho mines for a short time in 1863. He ran a freight line from The Dalles to Boise and then operated The Dalles to Canyon City Stage Company for a year. He moved back to Albany and drove for the Oregon to California Stage Company. Later, he drove sheep to California. In 1871, he moved to Rhea Creek ten miles southwest of Heppner. He sold out in 1881 and moved to Heppner. He also ran a feed store and was a veterinary surgeon as well as a leading stockman. He was a school director, city marshall, and he also served for four years as Heppner's mayor. He married **MARY E. RHEA** in 1869. She was born September 22, 1851 and died June 20, 1892. Tom died in 1918. They are buried in the Heppner Cemetery.

WILLIAM H. ROYSE was born April 4, 1816. He founded the town of Dairyville, which later became the town of Hardman, in 1879. He died March 6, 1887 and is buried in the old Hardman Cemetery northwest of the town.

DAVID N. HARDMAN was born September 8, 1838 in Indiana. He crossed the plains to the Willamette Valley in 1852. He then came to Umatilla County and stayed there until 1869 when he moved to Waitsburg, Washington. In 1878 he moved to a mile and a half east of Hardman, but he then moved to Hardman in 1883. He laid out the town and set up a general merchandise business. He married Nancy Royse, the daughter of William and Elizabeth Royse in 1869 at Weston. The town of Hardman is named for David. He died August 30, 1893 and is buried in the Hardman IOOF Cemetery several miles north of the town.

BENJAMIN H. PARKER was born January 22, 1827 in Canada. He moved to Ohio and then to Colorado in 1859 to mine. He came to Oregon in 1862 and ran a freight outfit until 1876 when he started Parkers Mill in partnership with Peter Gleason. Ben married Ada M. Jones in 1898. She had come from Ohio and had been a teacher for 20 years in various towns, including Heppner. The Parkers ran the sawmill, a hotel, and a stage station for many years. They were on the pioneer road from Heppner and Hardman to the town of Monument. The mill and hotel burned down some time after 1917. Ben died February 27, 1903 and is buried in the Hardman IOOF Cemetery.

PETER GLEASON was born on January 26, 1829 and died June 1, 1901. He too is buried in the Hardman IOOF Cemetery. He was Ben Parker's partner in establishing the sawmill at Parkers Mill.

ALBERT PETER LOVGREN was born March 29, 1824. His wife was **JOHANNA SOPHIA LOVGREN**, who was born in 1842. The Lovgrens were early pioneer settlers in the Hale Ridge area between Heppner and Condon. Albert died on September 7, 1896 and Johanna in 1907. They are in the Hardman IOOF Cemetery.

ALBERT WRIGHT was born January 12, 1825. His wife was **JULIA A. BARRY**, who was born October 22, 1827. They crossed the plains in 1853 to Clackamas County. They moved to three miles north of Hardman in 1872. Their son, **ANSON E. WRIGHT**, was born February 10, 1860 in Clackamas County. He married **IDA J. KNIGHTEN** in 1886. Ida was born in 1866. Anson expanded his father's holdings to 6000 acres and 6000 sheep. Anson Wright State Park west of Hardman is named for him. Albert died September 16, 1906 and Julia on December 9, 1903. They are buried in the Heppner Cemetery. Anson died in 1936 and Ida

in 1925. They are buried in the Hardman IOOF Cemetery.

EDWARD W. KILCUP was born in Nova Scotia about 1820. He was a sailor and then a miner in California. He moved to Puget Sound and ran a dairy. He married **EMMA LUCKMAN** in 1863 or 1869 in California. She was born May 4, 1839 in Warickshire, England. They settled on the North Fork of Little Butter Creek in 1880 and had a stage station at their place. Their daughter, Ada, built the Lena store and post office. Ed died August 27, 1887, aged 67 years. Emma died January 25, 1913. Ed and Emma are in the Heppner Cemetery.

HENRY PADBERG was born February 10, 1833 in Germany. He married **MARTHA V. RIGGS**, who was born on November 19, 1849. She was from Iowa. They came to Rhea Creek in 1870, the first settlers in their area. Martha died November 30, 1890 and Henry on October 23, 1911. They are in the Lexington Cemetery.

JOSIAH S. BOOTHBY was born October 24, 1824 in Ohio. He moved to Illinois and was a cabin boy on the Mississippi River. He arrived in Kansas in 1849, then moved on to Missouri. He returned to Illinois in 1861. During the Civil War, he was in Company F, 7th Missouri Infantry where he fought in 22 battles. After the war, he went to Kansas, and in 1879 he moved to Monmouth, Oregon. In 1883 he moved to Lexington and raised wheat and cattle. He was elected to the State Legislature in 1894. In 1899, he sold the farm and moved into the town of Lexington. He married Elizabeth Peyton in Illinois in 1844. She died in 1867. He married Susan J. Yates in 1867. Josiah died August 17, 1905 and is in the Lexington Cemetery.

THOMAS MARLATT and brother, Wesley, settled on Hinton Creek at the site of the present Heppner fairgrounds in the early 1860's. Tom was born in 1837 and died in 1914. He is buried in the Heppner Cemetery.

ANDREW ROOD was born January 22, 1843. His wife was **MILLIE TERRESSA ROOD**, who was born April 1, 1861. They were the pioneer settlers in Rood Canyon northwest of Hardman. Millie died May 28, 1913 and Andrew on March 16, 1920. They have a large eight foot monument in the

Heppner Cemetery. Andrew's twin brother was **EDWARD D. ROOD,** who was a veteran of the Civil War in Company H, 3 Wisconsin. Ed's wife was **LUTICIA ROOD.** She was born August 3, 1854 and perished in the Heppner Flood of June 14, 1903. Ed died November 1, 1918. They too are in the Heppner Cemetery.

The greatest disaster to ever hit the town of Heppner was the flash flood of June 14, 1903.

About 250 people out of a population of 1100 died as a result of this flood. The tombstones in the Heppner Cemetery show many examples of this disaster. One of the many tragedies occurred to the E. G. Ashbaugh family. The wife **CORA MAY ASHBAUGH,** and their seven children died in the flood. Cora was born July 8, 1872. The ages of the children were from just under eleven years to one month.

Chapter 11

Pioneers Of The Pilot Rock Area

As early as 1862, Pilot Rock was on several important routes that carried freight from Umatilla Landing (now Umatilla) to the gold mines of Baker and Granite areas. Ranchers also arrived in the 1860's, so the area became a very early important trade center.

ANDREW JACKSON STURTEVANT opened a store in the area in the 1860's. In 1871 he bought land from William Knotts and established his store at the present site of Pilot Rock. Andrew was born on November 14, 1832. He had been a teacher in the Willamette Valley before he loaded his possessions into a wheelbarrow and started for the gold mines of Eastern Oregon. He never got any farther than what later became Pilot Rock. Andrew married **CARRIE KNOTTS**, the daughter of William and **RACHEL KNOTTS**. She was born November 6, 1849 and died March 16, 1910. Andrew died in 1919. The Sturtevants are buried in the Pilot Rock Cemetery.

Rachel Knotts was born on October 12, 1810 and died December 14, 1865. Apparently, she and her husband, William, owned the land where Pilot Rock became established. It is not known when they first arrived in the area. She and her sons, **ISAAC KNOTTS** and **PERRY KNOTTS** are buried in the Pilot Rock Cemetery.

ISAAC KNOTTS was born on March 13, 1838 in Pennsylvania. (The date on his tombstone in 1830.) He moved with his parents to Virginia in 1842, and in 1844 migrated to Iowa. They came to Oregon City in 1853. In 1857, Isaac moved to some place in Umatilla County to farm and mine. He was so successful that in 1865 he bought 6000 acres on East Birch Creek south of Pilot Rock and raised sheep. He married **MARY SHILIFOE** in 1862. She was born on May 16, 1848. She was part Indian and was from French Prairie, Oregon. Isaac died August 11, 1904 and Mary on June 24, 1920.

PERRY O. KNOTTS was born in 1840. He married **FELICITA SHILIFOE**, the sister of Mary Shilifoe who married Perry's brother, Isaac. She was born on December 13, 1854 and died on February 15, 1914. Perry died in 1932.

Author Larry Nielsen lived on the original Isaac Knotts' place about a dozen years. In the 1930's, some of the original buildings were still standing. Perry Knotts' ranch was about half a mile farther up Birch Creek at the mouth of California Gulch. Author Don Galbreath's parents, the Sam Galbreaths, lived on the Perry Knotts place from 1918 to 1930.

ELI STEWART and wife, **ANNE C. STEWART**, were very early settlers in the Pilot Rock area. He was born August 13, 1813 in Ohio. He was a tailor by trade. Anne was born on May 20, 1814 in Kentucky. They were married in 1838. They moved to Iowa and in 1850 the family crossed the plains by ox team to Portland where he opened a tailor shop. They came to the Pilot Rock area in 1860—the first settlers in the area. Their son, **HAROLD STEWART**, was born on December 14, 1844 in Illinois. Harold married **MARY C. POMEROY** in 1875. (On her tombstone, she is Mary Dina Stewart.) Mary was born on February 20, 1857. Harold stayed with his parents until 1876 when he took a squatter's rights on Stewart Creek east of Pilot Rock. He moved to Pilot Rock in 1878 to operate a livery stable until 1898. He built the Pilot Rock Hotel. Eli died October 11, 1900, Anne on February 10, 1886, Harold on August 16, 1929, and Mary on October 9, 1917. All are buried in the Pilot Rock Cemetery.

JAMES M. HEMPHILL was born June 6, 1832 in New Hampshire. He moved to New York, and later at the age of 21, to California. He arrived in Portland in 1859. He came to Umatilla County in 1860 to prospect. He then freighted from The Dalles to the gold mines in Idaho. In 1865 he took squatter's rights near Pilot Rock just after he married **ELIZABETH RAMSBOTTOM**. They raised sheep as well as chickens and vegetables for the miners in the Granite region. Their sons, Alfred and Carl, became prominent citizens of Pilot Rock. James died July 3, 1912 and Elizabeth on November 14, 1926. They are buried in the Pilot Rock Cemetery.

ALEXANDER WAUGH was born October 31, 1826 in Indiana. He ran boats on the Mississippi River for some time before moving to Illinois to farm when he was 25. After eleven years, he came to East Birch Creek near Pilot Rock about 1863. He married **AGNES P. LITTLEPAGE** in 1852. They farmed and sold garden truck to miners and later moved to West Birch Creek and raised stock. Mr. Waugh died on March 16, 1907. Agnes was born in February 1827 and died June 8, 1900. They share a tombstone in the Pilot Rock Cemetery.

ABRAM MILLER was born April 30, 1838 in Indiana. He moved to Iowa when 16. In 1862 he crossed the plains by ox team. He had married **NANCY MOORE** in 1860. They settled at the present site of Pendleton in 1863. They sold out to Moses Goodwin in 1864. They came to Pilot Rock where they raised several children who became well known in the area. Daughter, Austie (Austa) Alice became the wife of J. W. Arrasmith of Colfax and Pullman, Washington. Hattie M. became Mrs. Lewis Roy, the blacksmith at Pilot Rock. Ida married John Royer, the operator of the Pilot Rock Hotel. Nancy was born on May 11, 1840 and died on June 17, 1890. Abram died on May 31, 1913. They are buried in the Pilot Rock Cemetery.

CHARLES OGILVY was born September 1845 and his wife, **CATHERINE OGILVY**, on May 23, 1852. They raised cattle and sheep near the headwaters of California Gulch, a branch of East Birch Creek. He was a Scottish stone mason, and he built a beautiful stone cellar on his place. They had 14 children. They had a dispute with Lee Dale over the boundary between their properties. On June 3, 1915, Lee returning home drunk, shot both Charles and Catherine. Catherine was killed instantly, but Charles survived long enough to leave a note stat-

ing that they had been shot by Lee Dale. Charles died on June 4, 1915. Dale was sentenced to life imprisonment but was later paroled. In the late 1920's, the author hiked into the Ogilvy place. Blood stains were still visible on the porch. By 1980, the house was gone. Only part of the once beautiful stone cellar remained.

ELEAZAR "ELI" GILLIAM was born December 3, 1840 in Missouri. In 1847 he crossed the plains with his family to Polk County near Dallas. He drove their sheep on the trip. Eli married **NANCY JANE ROBBINS** in 1861. She was born on May 8, 1842 in Indiana and was a direct descendent of Nancy Hanks, the mother of Abraham Lincoln. Her family came to near Salem in 1852 but later moved to Molalla in the early 1860's. In 1863 Eli and Nancy Jane moved to the Meadows near Echo. In 1865 they settled on East Birch Creek four miles south of Pilot Rock. They had bought out a squatter for a horse and $75. Eli and Nancy Jane had eleven children. They did most of their trading at Umatilla Landing—hauling wool one way and supplies on the return trip. During the 1870's and 1880's Eli conducted singing schools in Alta (later Pilot Rock), Pendleton, The Meadows, and Umatilla. Eli was Justice of the Peace for many years and also assessor of Umatilla County. He discovered the famous Ben Harrison Goldmine near Granite. His son, Albert, operated the mine for many years. Eli died of Bright's disease on March 15, 1902. Nancy Jane died March 29, 1929. They are buried in the Olney Cemetery at Pendleton surrounded by many of their children.

When the author lived on the original Isaac Knotts place, the Gilliam farm joined us to the north. The author, Larry Nielsen, vaguely remembers Nancy Jane, but he knew the son, **ALBERT**, and daughter, **ELLA McBROOM**, very well. Albert lived next door to us to the south for several years. Larry delivered milk to the Gilliams in a two quart lard pail for ten cents. Another daughter of Eli and Nancy Jane was **GRACE GILLIAM**. She furnished most of the money to build Grace Hospital in Pilot Rock where both of the authors were born. Grace was also treasurer of Umatilla County. Most of the Gilliams and McBrooms are buried in the Olney Cemetery in Pendleton.

Chapter 12
Umatilla County Pioneers

JOHN S. GURDANE was born May 4, 1824 at sea on the way from Scotland to the United States. He was in New York and Canada. In 1846 he was the captain of a merchant marine ship in the US Navy. It sank in a gale in 1859. In the Civil War, he was in Company E, 14th Wisconsin Infantry. He fought at Shiloh, Vicksburg, and was on Sherman's march to the sea. He moved to Missouri in 1866 where he farmed and railroaded. In 1882 he crossed the plains to Pendleton. Later he went to the area of Gurdane, which is named for him. Today, Gurdane is a ghost town on a back road between Ukiah and Pilot Rock. After 17 years of raising cattle, the Gurdanes moved to Pendleton. In 1894 John was elected to the State Legislature. After his first wife died, John married CELIA E. McBROOM in 1867. She was born February 18, 1840 and died April 20, 1919. John died October 16, 1920. They share a large pink granite tombstone in Pendleton's Olney Cemetery.

DR. JOHN TEEL was born April 6, 1806 in Toledo, Ohio. Other sources say Pennsylvania. He inherited a plantation in Louisiana but later gave the place to his 13 slaves. He was a doctor in New York. He moved to Kansas, and in 1860 the family took oxen to Oregon and settled at Echo. In 1861 the government appointed him to be the first doctor to the Indians on the Umatilla Indian Reservation. In 1877 he co-discovered what is now Lehman Springs. Dr. Teel moved to Pendleton. His daughter, Nancy Jane Teel married Olney McCoy, a freighter. McCoy was killed by Indians during the Bannock War of 1878 on Imigrant Hill at Deadman Pass. Dr. Teel was the first elected superintendent of schools of Umatilla County. Dr. Teel died February 27, 1880 and is buried at Pendleton.

JAMES LEHMAN was born July 17, 1831. He discovered Lehman Springs with Dr. John Teel. He made the springs into a resort. James died October 10, 1913 and is buried in Pendleton's Olney Cemetery.

JAMES R. DANIEL was born October 18, 1826 in Pennsylvania. He went to the US Naval Academy and was in the Mexican War in 1846. He mined in California in 1848 and then went to Australia to mine. He mined on the Fraser River in Canada in 1858 and made a fortune. He showed up in San Francisco and Portland. In 1858 or 1859 he drove cattle to Umatilla County. He built a hotel at Rieth and one at Meacham which he sold to A. B. Meacham. In 1862, he married CATHERINE MESSINGER. Her family had arrived from Indiana that year. James farmed and raised stock, and in 1889 moved to Pendleton. James died September 29, 1901. Catherine died in 1878. The Daniels are in the Pendleton Cemetery.

JOHN L. GULLIFORD was born July 2, 1836 in Illinois. At age 16 he arrived in Lane County. He fought in the Rogue River War. He moved to Klickatat County, Washington and then back to Lane County in 1866. He moved to the Butter Creek area in 1872. His wife was JULIA A. GULLIFORD who was born on August 6, 1845. They moved to a fruit farm near Milton in 1894. John died there on February 7, 1896 according to his tombstone. Another source says he died in 1899. Julia died June 7, 1920. They are buried in the Olney Cemetery in Pendleton.

AURA M. MORSE was born August 23, 1829. She married Moses E. Goodwin in 1846. They took ox teams to the Vancouver area, but in 1864 they settled at the site of Pendleton. They built the original Pendleton Hotel and a bridge across the Umatilla River. Moses died in January 1871, and Aura married Henry J. Raley in 1872. Aura died

July 21, 1913 and is buried in the Pendleton Cemetery.

JAMES H. KOONTZ was born May 2, 1830 in the Buckeye state. He moved to Iowa and then to Portland by ox team. He moved to Umatilla Landing in 1863. There he ran a general merchandise business that supplied goods to miners in Idaho and eastern Oregon. He was postmaster of Umatilla. His first wife was Elizabeth W. Williams. His second wife was **CYNTHIA ANN HYATT**, who was born January 2, 1837. James laid out the town of Echo in 1881. He built a flour mill there, and ran a general store. The town was named for their daughter, **ECHO KOONTZ**, who was born November 5, 1877. Echo was a talented musician who studied at the Boston Conservatory. There she met Charles Miller, an Englishman. After they were married they returned to Echo where Charles ran a store. James, Cynthia, and Echo are buried in the Echo Cemetery. James died January 31, 1912, Cynthia on April 11, 1930, and Echo on August 18, 1908. The James Koontz home is still being used in Echo.

ROBERT NELSON STANFIELD was born in Illinois on December 3, 1832. He moved to California when he was 17 years of age. He mined and made enough money to buy a ranch and raise cattle. About 1860 he moved to Umatilla and freighted. He married **PHOEBE M. ATWOOD** in 1865. She was born November 6, 1850 and had crossed the plains to near Hermiston in 1863. Phoebe died November 3, 1871, and Robert married Hattie Townsend in 1873. They moved to Pendleton in 1883 and ran a warehouse. Robert was the first sheriff of Umatilla County after the county seat was moved to Pendleton. They moved to Butter Creek in 1885. Robert died April 15, 1896 and is buried with Phoebe in the Echo Cemetery.

CAPTAIN ROBERT B. RANDALL was born in England in 1819. He came to the United States and joined the Corps of Engineers. His job in 1874 was to remove hazards from the Umatilla Rapids. In the Umatilla Cemetery, he found the grave of his English sweetheart, Emma Louise Tucker (1830-1863). She had married and came to the Umatilla area, but Robert had lost track of her. He expressed his wish to be buried by his sweetheart when he died. On March 7, 1875, Robert drowned in the Columbia River. His marker in Umatilla Cemetery is broken and lying on the ground. No trace of Emma's tombstone has been found. Is this a true story with Robert being buried by Emma, or is this a fairy tale? This mystery is left for others to solve.

Weston is the second oldest town in Umatilla County. Weston was founded by **THOMAS TYNDALL LIEUALLEN** in 1862. (One source says the year was 1865.) Thomas was born in 1825. His wife was **SARAH E. LIEUALLEN**. She was born in 1840 and died in 1924. Tom died in 1885. Their tombstone in the Kees Cemetery near Weston has been toppled over.

JAMES W. FROOME was born December 11, 1819 in Ontario, Canada. He married **JANET IRVING** there in 1848. He was a sailor on the St. Lawrence River. They came to California in 1860 and to Walla Walla in 1876 then to Athena in 1879. James built the first hotel in Athena. Janet was born on October 27, 1829 and died on October 9, 1893. James died on February 26, 1901. They are buried in the Athena Cemetery.

The town of Athena is built on the land first settled by **THOMAS J. KIRK**. He was born August 12, 1839. His wife was **ANNE KIRK,** who was born on October 19, 1839. Tom died January 26, 1910 and Anne on September 17, 1907. They are buried in the Athena Cemetery. **ALEX KIRK,** who probably was Tom's father is also buried there. He was born February 8, 1805 and died March 19, 1877.

DARWIN A. RICHARDS was born December 2, 1828 in New York. He moved to California in 1850 and mined for seven years. He came to Portland and then moved to The Dalles where he ran a livery stable. He also freighted to Boise. He was thrown from a wagon and run over. This accident left him crippled for life. Later, he settled at the mouth of McKay Creek. He was the first appointed clerk of Umatilla County in 1862. In 1866 he moved to Athena and established the Richards Stage Station. In 1878 he helped establish Athena, which was then known as Centerville. He married Maria Louise Meader in 1879. Darwin died May 27, 1901 and is buried in the Athena Cemetery.

ALEXANDER PATTERSON was born February 14, 1808. In the spring of 1876 the family started from the Kansas City area and settled at Gurdane. Along with Alexander and his wife were their son John L. and his wife. He worked at William Beasley's sawmill while living in Gurdane. Later the family moved to Long Creek where son John built the "Old House." The elegant "Old House" still stands. Alexander is in an isolated grave in the center of Gurdane.

DR. WILLIAM MCKAY was born in Astoria in 1824 and died in Pendleton in 1893. He was a physician and soldier. Several places have been named for him—McKay Creek north of Prineville and also McKay Creek and Dam between Pendleton and Pilot Rock. In 1866 or January 1867 he headed a troop of Indian scouts camped on McKay Creek in Crook County. He was the step-grandson of Dr. John McLaughlin, his father having been raised by him.

Chapter 13

Union County Pioneers

FRED NODINE became one of the founders of the town of Union when he settled there in June 1862. He started the first orchard and nursery. He sold wild hay to pack trains in the winter for $100 a ton. He also ran cattle. A better route was needed for pack trains from Walla Walla across the Grande Ronde Valley to the mines around Baker City and beyond. Dr. D. S. Baker, a merchant in Walla Walla, hired Nodine and Three Fingered Smith to establish a new route across the Grande Ronde Valley to the Powder River Valley for a price of $200 in 1862. They built a crossing over the Grande Ronde River and marked the route by placing a stake in the ground every mile across the valley and up Pyles Canyon. In two weeks, there were 10 pack trains of 20 to 30 animals ready to use the trail. These animals left a well marked trail for others to follow with very little effort from Nodine and his partner! Nodine was a kind-hearted fellow who donated the land for the Union Cemetery and money to many friends. Author Larry Nielsen's brother, Frank, lives on part of Nodine's property. Fred Nodine was born in 1826 and died in 1907. His wife, ELIZA NODINE, was born in 1841 and died in 1923. Their grave in the Union Cemetery is marked by a large five foot tall granite block.

JOEL D. CARROLL was born October 14, 1818. He married MIRANDA (MARANDA on tombstone) BENNETT in 1840 in Indiana. She was born on January 17, 1825. Joel was a blacksmith. They moved to Iowa and lived there until 1864 when they came to Union by ox team. He was county treasurer from 1878 to 1882. The Carrolls had ten children. Miranda died June 18, 1897, and Joel died August 5, 1910. They are buried in the Union Cemetery.

SIMON MILLER was born in Switzerland on April 4, 1832. He came to western Oregon, and in 1863 moved to Union. He married JULIET A. GAL-LOWAY in 1858. She was born on October 3, 1841 in Indiana and subsequently moved to Columbia County, Oregon. She died on February 8, 1885. Simon died on October 28, 1887. They each have a seven foot obelisk in the Union Cemetery.

DAVIS W. JOHNSON was born in Indiana on April 22, 1824. He was in the military during the early part of the Civil War. He married MARGARET C. BELL, who was born on August 8, 1825. Johnson came to the Willamette Valley in 1863 and onto Union County in 1864. Margaret died on June 2, 1892 and Davis on May 1, 1910. They are buried in the Union Cemetery.

JOHN T. OUTHOUSE was born on November 15, 1828. In 1852, he became Oregon's first free public school teacher. Before that time, the parents of children had to pay teachers to educate their children. The public at first did not have to pay property taxes to support schools in Oregon. Later, John moved to Union County and continued to teach. He became superintendent of schools for Union County. Mr. Outhouse pronounced his name about like Otis. He died on October 29, 1889. He has a large nine foot monument in the Union Cemetery.

JAMES M. PYLE was born on December 26, 1829. A few years after Fred Nodine established a pack trail up what is now known as Pyle's Canyon in 1862, James Pyle built a toll road up the canyon. The road which was completed in 1865, was a very important route for supplies to the mines around Baker City and Idaho from such places as Umatilla Landing and Walla Walla. Pyle's road continued to be a toll road until the county purchased it in 1869 or 1870. Pyle became a county judge in 1863, and in 1864 was elected to the State Senate. Pyle died on June 17, 1867 and is buried in the Union Cemetery.

BLADON (BLADEN on tombstone) ASHBY settled at Pyles Canyon in 1877 with his wife, Sarah.

He fought in the Civil War in Company K, 6th Iowa Infantry. Beside his tombstone in the Union Cemetery is a GAR (Grand Army of the Republic) marker. He died June 24, 1900, but the tombstone gives no date of birth. This is an annoying custom of not giving dates on the tombstones of Civil War veterans.

ADNA C. CRAIG was born on September 14, 1821 in Ohio. He was a bricklayer by trade. In 1849 he got the goldbug and left for California in hopes of getting rich. In 1861, he travelled to Idaho again in search of gold. He then operated a packing business between Umatilla and Idaho. In 1871 he married **AMELIA (DRUMM) RICE,** and in the same year, they moved to Union County to farm. He was sheriff for several years, a county judge for eight years, and county assessor. In 1884, he built the Depot Hotel. Adna died on November 24, 1900. Amelia died September 11, 1914. They are buried in the Union Cemetery.

J. E. DAVIS was born on May 21, 1826, and his wife, **R. (ROMAINE) A. DAVIS** on June 10, 1831. They came to Union County in 1876 and farmed four miles north of North Powder. Their son, **E. W. DAVIS,** ran a flour mill. The son married **ADELIA E. DAVIS** in 1882. J. E. Davis died March 30, 1885, and his wife on November 15, 1898. E. W. died in 1936, and Adelia in 1902. Both E. W. and Adelia were born in 1861. All of the Davis family is buried in Union Cemetery.

ABEL ELSWORTH EATON was born May 20, 1834 in New Hampshire. He moved to Indiana, Ohio, and Illinois. He was a school teacher. He crossed the plains to Baker City in 1862. He cut 40 tons of wild hay with a scythe to sell to packers. Anyone who has used a scythe knows what a tremendous amount of work this was! He started a freighting business with 100 yoke of oxen and two six-mule teams. He settled in the Grande Ronde Valley to farm in 1867. In that same year, he married **MARY E. BAIRD.** She died after 27 years of marriage on December 6, 1894 at the age of 43 years, 7 months, and 5 days. About 1871, Abel started a woolen mill at Union. He was one of the mayors of Union. Abel died January 15, 1917. He

and Mary each have elaborately carved ten foot monuments in the Union Cemetery.

WILLIAM ROTH was born on January 23, 1834 in Germany. He came to Ohio at 18 years of age. He moved to Iowa and then crossed the plains to Union in 1864. He was a carpenter by trade and was responsible for the construction of many buildings in Union. He likewise purchased considerable property in town. He owned a large stock ranch 40 miles north of Huntington along the Snake River. As a result of his rather vast holdings he became a wealthy man. He died on March 17, 1911 and has a large granite monument four feet high in the Union Cemetery.

NICHOLAS TARTER was born in the Prussian Rheinprovince in Germany. His wife was **A. M. TARTER.** They eventually arrived at North Powder where he started a flour mill in 1872. This mill was the first industry in the town. Nicholas died on October 2, 1899 at an age of 77 years, 3 months, and 8 days. Mrs. Tarter died on January 19, 1907 at an age of 77 years, 10 months, and 26 days. They share an unusual nine foot monument in the Union Cemetery.

GREEN ARNOLD was born on May 17, 1818 in New York. He migrated to California in 1850 but returned to Michigan in 1851. He came to Milwaukie, Oregon in 1852 and operated a hotel. His next move was to Champoeg for a short time before taking a pack train of trade goods for Indians to the Butter Creek area. In October 1853 he returned to Champoeg, but 1854 found him running a trading post at the foot of Ladd Canyon in Union County. He was appointed an Indian agent and was at the Utilla Agency at the present site of Echo until 1855 when he moved to The Dalles area and farmed on Threemile Creek. In 1857 he moved to the mouth of Birch Creek and was one of the first white men to settle in the Pendleton area. He raised the first wheat in that region. His restless nature would not let him farm very long. So, in 1862 Green Arnold, along with Daniel Chaplin and several other pioneers, became the first settlers in La Grande. He had retained the trading post at Ladd Canyon. Some people credit him with giving La Grande its name. Green Arnold died November 14, 1893 at an age of 76 years, 5 months, and 27 days. He and relatives have a nine foot monument in the La Grande Grandview Cemetery.

DANIEL CHAPLIN was born in 1823 in New York. He moved to Michigan and in 1853 married **HANNAH ARNOLD**, a sister of Green Arnold. They crossed the plains to the Walla Walla Valley in 1854 and in Dayton, Washington he built a warehouse. In 1861 or '62, they along with Green Arnold and others became the first settlers at La Grande. Daniel ran the Land Office in La Grande and was elected to the State Legislature. He died on December 9, 1888, aged 65 years, 3 months, 6 days. Hannah died March 25, 1905, aged 81 years, 6 months, and 6 days. Daniel and Hannah share the same monument with Green Arnold in the La Grande Grandview Cemetery.

The Rinehart family was one of the earliest settlers, and most prominent citizens, in this part of eastern Oregon. **LEWIS BIRD RINEHART, SR.** was born on September 5, 1801. His wife was **ELIZABETH RINEHART**. She was born February 19, 1808. They had lived in Illinois and moved to Iowa in 1846. They crossed the plains to near Eugene in 1854. In 1863 they moved to the site of present Summerville. They built the first building there, and gave the town its name. Lewis died December 10, 1881, and Elizabeth on January 30, 1903. They are buried in the Summerville Cemetery.

LEWIS BIRD RINEHART, JR. was their son. He was born April 8, 1844 in Illinois. In 1862, Lewis and two brothers moved from the Eugene area to Summerville. He bought a flour mill in 1866 and ran it for three years. He freighted by ox team from Summerville to the mines at Idaho City. In 1868 Lewis brought the first cattle to the Malheur River near the Washoe Ferry on the Snake River. In 1869 he bought into J. L. Morrow's mercantile business in La Grande. He was elected treasurer of Union County in 1870. Also, in 1870 he bought the Keeney Station at Vale. He moved to Vale in 1872 and built the famous stone house as a home and hostelry. The hotel was opened January 1, 1873 by a grand ball hosted by his wife, Amelia (Glenn) Rinehart, who he married in 1867. Lewis operated a ferry at Vale from 1872 to 1881 when he sold out and moved to Baker County. For a period he was

assessor of Baker County. In 1884 he was elected to the State Senate. The Rineharts moved back to Union where they went into the real estate business in addition to operating the stock ranch near Vale. Lewis died on March 18, 1909 and is buried in the Union Cemetery.

WILLIAM H. PATTON was born October 2, 1812. His wife, **ELIZABETH PATTON** was born December 6, 1827. They settled at Summerville in 1857 and ran the stage station on the Thomas-Ruckel Road. William named the town after a friend, Alexander Sommerville, but the name was changed to Summerville. Elizabeth died March 9, 1872 and William on February 19, 1892. Their graves are in the Summerville Cemetery.

JOSEPH HARRIS was born in North Carolina on March 19, 1821 or 1824. (His tombstone gives the date of 1821.) His family moved to West Virginia in 1826 and on to Missouri. During the Civil War, Joseph was in Company K, 42nd Missouri Volunteer Infantry. In 1865 he took the Oregon Trail to six miles south of Elgin where he farmed. He married **MARY A. STURGILL** in Virginia in 1840. She was born in 1819. Mary died November 8, 1888 and Joe in 1912. They are buried in the Summerville Cemetery. Mount Harris in the northeast edge of the Grande Ronde Valley is named for them.

BENJAMIN BROWN was born January 18, 1831 in England. He came to Michigan in 1857 and to California, by way of Panama, in 1858. He went to the Fraser mines in Canada and then back to Michigan in 1860 to get his wife, **FRANCES KIRK**, whom he had married in England in 1852. She was born July 28, 1826. Together, they crossed the plains by ox team in 1860 to Umatilla County. He freighted while his wife ran a boarding house on the Umatilla Indian Reservation. In 1861, he and nine others, moved to within a few miles of La Grande and in 1862, to present La Grande where he built the first house in town. He plowed the first land in Union County and later became County Assessor. The Browns also operated a hotel, farmed and raised stock. Benjamin, the founder of La Grande, died September 12, 1909, and his wife Frances died on February 21, 1910. The Browns are buried in the Island City Cemetery.

Chapter 14

Baker County Pioneers

Most of the history of Baker County started on October 23, 1861 when **HENRY H. GRIFFIN** discovered gold on Griffin Gulch near Baker City. He had come to Oregon from the mines in California. He, three friends from California, and a number of Oregonians started across Eastern Oregon to look for the legendary Blue Bucket Mine. This mine had been discovered by Meek's Lost Wagon Train of 1845. The discovery of large quantities of gold in the area around Griffin Gulch started a great gold rush and the founding of the town of Auburn. By 1862, there were 5,000 to 10,000 mines at Auburn. Henry H. Griffin died on January 3, 1883 at an age of 59 years. His tombstone is one of the few in the Auburn Cemetery. His name is misspelled on the tombstone.

DAVID S. LITTLEFIELD was in the party with Henry Griffin that discovered gold in the Auburn area in October 1861. He was born in Maine on September 27, 1829. He went to California to mine in 1850. In 1858 he went to the mines of the Frazer River in Canada. He returned to California and joined the party that discovered gold on Griffin Gulch. News of their discovery leaked out when Dave and another member of the party went to Walla Walla to get supplies. He later quit mining and raised horses in the Auburn area. In 1872 he married the widow **MARY A. GRANT**. Her first husband was Dr. Grant who established the first drug store in Baker County. Mary was born in England on October 15, 1836. David died on January 19, 1913 and Mary on October 14, 1913. They are buried in the Baker Mt. Hope Cemetery.

WILLIAM H. PACKWOOD was born on October 23, 1832 in Illinois. He enlisted in the Army in 1848, and the next year he was sent to California. In 1850, Packwood came to Oregon by ship but returned to California the next year. He was shipwrecked near Port Orford, Oregon on January 3, 1852. He was discharged from the army in 1853 and took up mining. He enlisted in the army again and served as a captain during the Yakima Indian War of 1855-56. In 1857, Packwood was a delegate to the Oregon constitutional convention. He started raising cattle. In 1862 he took supplies and cattle to the mines. He was a founder of the town of Auburn and prominent in the construction of the Auburn Ditch which supplied water for the placer mines in the area. Later, he was the promoter and leading figure in the construction of the Eldorado Ditch, the Sanger Ditch, and the Sparta Ditch. These ditches supplied water to the mines in other areas of Northeastern Oregon. (The story of the 136 mile long Eldorado Ditch is told in the author's book, *In The Ruts Of The Wagon Wheels*.) Packwood had his finger and money in many other projects including mines at Sanger, a boarding house in Sparta, and a ferry on the Snake River. Packwood married **JOHANNA A. O'BRIEN**, who started the first school in Auburn in 1862. She was born on June 25, 1842. Mr. Packwood was the first Baker County school superintendent, and in 1888 was elected recorder of Baker City. William's great grandson is Oregon's U.S. Senator, Robert Packwood. William died on September 1, 1917, and Johanna died on October 14, 1926. They are buried in Baker Mount Hope Cemetery.

HARDIN W. ESTES was born November 2, 1828 in Missouri. When he was 18, he joined the army and helped establish army posts from the Missouri River to The Dalles. He went to California in 1849 and struck it rich by mining for gold. He was in Oregon in 1853. Later, he helped construct stage stations for Ben Holliday from Carson City, Nevada to Salt Lake City. He started for the Idaho mines but stopped in Baker County in June 1862 when he learned of the gold strike at Auburn. He built the first bridge across the Powder River and charged the miners a toll. On June 16, 1862 Hardin established the first farm in Baker County near North Powder. He sold fruit and vegetables to the miners as well as hay for their horses. He later moved to Baker City. He had married Mahali Ring in 1851. His second wife was **PERLINA (or PEARLINA) SMITH** whom he married in 1867. She was born March 19, 1835. Hardin was a county commissioner for four years. Perlina died on September 15, 1908 and Hardin on June 2, 1910. They are in the Baker Cemetery.

EDWARD P. CRANSTON was born in 1836. He arrived at Auburn in June 1862 and set up a store. Ed and William Packwood were two of the pioneers who laid out the town of Auburn. He later moved to near Keating. His wife was **ANNA E. CRANSTON**, who was born in 1845. The Cranston Ditch near Keating is named for their son, Herbert. Ed died in 1903 and Anna in 1932. They, and many of their children and relatives, share an eight foot monument with a cross at the top, in the Baker Cemetery.

JAMES H. SHINN was born in Terre Haute, Indiana on August 23, 1836. He arrived in Baker County in 1862 and eventually became the sheriff in 1870. He also served as the county judge. His wife was **LAVINA SHINN** who was born in 1850. James died on December 30, 1889. After James died, she married a Mr. Wisdom. Lavina died in 1943. The Shinns are buried in the Baker Cemetery.

LUTHER B. ISON was born October 19, 1841 in Kentucky. He came to the Baker City area in 1862. He became a wealthy lawyer and business man. He was a teacher and became superintendent of schools in 1869. He was county clerk in 1870. He became a judge and district attorney. In 1882 he was elected to the state legislature. He married Josephine Cates in 1870. Luther died on December 28, 1889. He is buried with his daughter, **BERTHA ISON** in the Baker Cemetery. Bertha died on September 7, 1891. The elegant Ison home still stands in Baker City and is now the home of Bank of America.

HIRAM OSBORN was born in 1803 or 1809. He came to Wingville in either 1862 or 1864 from Missouri. He raised cattle and farmed. He was elected Baker County assessor in 1868. His son, Stephen, drove ox teams pulling freight wagons from the Columbia River to the mines of eastern Oregon when he was only 15 years old! Hiram died November 26, 1888 and is buried in the Wingville Cemetery. His wife, **DRUCILLA OSBORN,** was born in Missouri on August 22, 1809. She died on February 16, 1888 and is buried in the Wingville Cemetery.

WILLIAM F. McCRARY was born February 21, 1824. He was the first postmaster of the mining town of Auburn. This was the first post office in northeastern Oregon. Later, in 1866, he was the postmaster of Baker City. His wife, **ELIZABETH E. McCRARY** was born on February 1, 1830. William died January 21, 1875 and his wife on June 6, 1880. They share a six foot pillar in the Baker Cemetery.

William N. (Doc) Anthony settled by the foothills of Baker Valley on Anthony Creek in 1862. He was the first doctor in the area. His homestead was on the pioneer Dealy Road between the Baker City area and Pilot Rock. A toll station was on the Anthony homestead. His wife was **SARAH A. ANTHONY.** She was born on March 19, 1829 and died on January 16, 1909. She has a small tombstone in the Baker Cemetery. William is supposed to be buried with his wife, but he has no tombstone.

Morrow County Pioneers

Cluff

Oliver Towner Petteys

Penland

Ashbaugh

Nancy Morrow

Joseph A. Woolery

Pioneers of the Pilot Rock Area and Umatilla County

Isaac Knotts

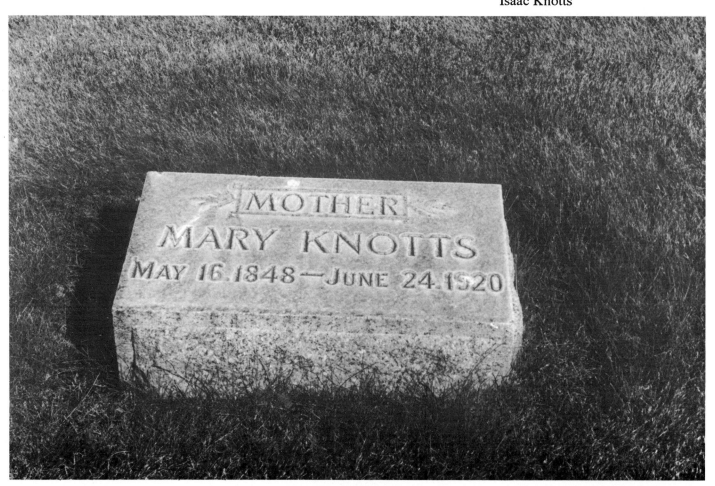

Mary Knotts

Alexander Patterson

Eleazar Gilliam

A. J. Sturtevant

Eli and Anne Stewart

William C. McKay

James R. Daniel

John Gurdane

Robert N. Stanfield

James H. Koontz

LIEUALLEN

HON. THOMAS T.
1825 —— 1885
HIS WIFE
SARAH E.
1840 —— 1924
AT REST

Thomas T. and Sarah E. Lieuallen

Union County Pioneers

Lewis and Elizabeth Rinehart

L. B. Rinehart

Joseph and Mary Harris

Eliza Gale

Green Arnold

Nodine

Nicolas Tarter

John Outhouse

Eaton

Baker County Pioneers

William H. Packwood

Joseph Gale

William Baldock

Wallowa County Pioneers

Jack Johnson

Joseph F. Johnson

Edward J. Renfrow

A. C. and Sarah A. Smith

Chapter 15

Wallowa County Pioneers

Wallowa County was not settled by white men until the 1870's. It was the ancestral home of the Nez Perce Indians, and white men were trespassers. However, large numbers of settlers began arriving in the Wallowa Valley in 1871. The Nez Perce Indians under Chief Joseph were finally driven out in 1877.

ANDERSON C. SMITH was born on August 16, 1831 in Illinois. He married **SARAH A. WHITTINGTON** in 1856. She was born on November 6, 1841 in Illinois. He retired as a cavalry lieutenant during the early Civil War period. He was in Company D, 9th Kansas Cavalry. Prior to that, he had gone to California in 1852 by ox team to mine. In 1856 he returned to Kansas. The Smiths then left Kansas with the Iowa Wagon Train in 1862 and settled in the Grande Ronde Valley. It is said that the Smiths were the first settlers at Cove. During the 1860's Anderson spent much time exploring what later became Wallowa County and earned the title "the Daniel Boone of Wallowa County." He spoke the Nez Perce language and spent the winter of 1868 in the Imnaha River region with his Indian friend, Yellow Hawk. He was the first to name numerous features of Wallowa County such as Hurricane Creek. He constructed the first road into Wallowa Valley between 1871 and 1873. His rugged, spectacular road descended Minam Hill, bridged the Wallowa River, and ascended steep Smith Mountain before it dropped down to the Wallowa Valley. (See this author's book *Roads Of Yesterday In Northeastern Oregon* for the story of this road.) Anderson charged a dollar toll per wagon to use his road and bridge. He sold the road in 1878 and moved to Alder Slope near the Enterprise of today. During the Bannock War of 1878, Smith was an interpreter for the army. Over the years, he had been studying law from books, and

in 1888 was admitted to the bar. In Enterprise he practiced law and raised horses. The Smiths had ten children. Smith Mountain is named after Anderson Smith.

Anderson had brought sheep into Wallowa County in 1873. He ran a stage line from Alder Slope to Lewiston, Idaho via Promise and Lost Prairie in the early 1880's. By 1896, the Smiths were living in Enterprise. A. C. Smith died on August 10, 1914 and Sarah on April 15, 1914. They are buried in the Enterprise Cemetery.

FRANCIS C. BRAMLET was born on June 26, 1827 in Georgia. He married **MARTHA E. TOWER** in 1867. She was born on May 25, 1844. Francis Bramlet's family moved to Tennessee when Francis was six. In 1843 they moved to Missouri and then came to Yamhill County in 1852. With the death of the parents, Francis had to care for three sisters and two brothers. From Yamhill County they moved to Coos County and then to Douglas County. He fought in the Rogue River War in 1855-56.

The Bramlets came with the first settlers to the Wallowa Valley and settled a few miles northwest of the present town of Wallowa in 1871. They brought the first sheep to Wallowa County. They also started the first post office in the county in 1874. Francis died on March 15, 1911 and Martha on October 14, 1913. They are buried in the Bramlet cemetery near where they settled.

JOSEPH F. JOHNSON was another of the first settlers in the Wallowa Valley in 1871. He was born on April 17, 1839 in Missouri. His family moved to Yamhill County when he was eight years old. Later, they moved to Douglas County. When Joseph was 20, he headed to the mines in British Columbia and then to Idaho. He returned to Yamhill and Douglas Counties to farm and do carpenter work. In 1871 he went to Wallowa Valley, built a cabin, and stocked it with food and firewood. He married **FANNIE APPLEGATE,** daughter of Charles Applegate, in 1871. She was born August 19, 1850. In 1872, the Johnsons returned to Wallowa Valley. Fannie carried their baby up Smith Mountain in the snow while Joe backpacked their home furnishings up the mountain. They had an unbroken team on their wagon, and Joe would not trust them on the steep slopes of Smith Mountain. When they reached their cabin, they found that their food and wood had been stolen. This situation forced Joe to make a quick trip to Summerville for food. On their farm three miles west of present Wallowa, they raised cattle, horses, and sheep. Their family consisted of eight children. Joe laid out the town of Wallowa and promoted its growth. Fannie died on February 23, 1923 and Joe on November 22, 1923. They are buried in the Bramlet Cemetery.

JOHN ZURCHER was one of the founders of Enterprise. He was born in Switzerland on October 19, 1837. He came to Ohio in 1852. During the Civil War, he was in Company I, 30th Ohio Volunteer Infantry. He was wounded in 1862. John was a carriage maker by trade. He moved to Montana in 1881. In 1882 he settled at the site of present Enterprise where he farmed and made carriages. He married Helen Hogan in Ohio in 1870. John and R. F. Stubblefield laid out the town of Enterprise in 1886. John died January 3, 1904 and is buried in the Enterprise Cemetery.

WINSLOW P. POWERS was born in Vermont on April 8, 1821. The family moved to Illinois in 1826. He came to the Willamette Valley in 1847. He was a carpenter and built some of the first buildings in Portland. He went to the California mines in 1849, but returned the same year and farmed near Albany until 1853 when he moved to Douglas County. He married **HARRIET N. TOWER** of Douglas County in 1854. The Powers had ten children. Their daughter, Viola, became the first person married in Wallowa County when she wed Henry Schaeffer. Harriet was born in Illinois on October 12, 1837. She crossed the plains to Oregon in 1853. The Powers moved to four miles north of the future town of Wallowa in 1872. Winslow assisted in organizing the first bank in Wallowa County at Joseph. Winslow died October 21, 1895 and Harriet on July 13, 1913. They are buried in the Bramlet Cemetery.

LEVI J. ROUSE was born on October 15, 1835 in Ohio. He became a teacher. He moved to Iowa in 1857. He took the Oregon Trail to the Willamette Valley in 1859. He drove cattle to California in 1860. He proceeded to the Idaho mines in 1861 and to the Grande Ronde Valley in 1864. He went to Idaho again but soon returned to Oregon where he taught school. In 1886 he came to Wallowa County and became its first superintendent of schools in 1887. He was county clerk for four terms. He was appointed postmaster of Enterprise in 1897 and also published a newspaper. He also owned a farm on Alder Slope. Earlier, Levi along with W. H. Odell ran the first surveys in Wallowa County. He died in 1907 and is buried in the Enterprise Cemetery.

JAMES A. WRIGHT was one of the first pioneers to settle near Joseph. He was born on either May 30 or 31, 1841 in Indiana. He moved to Kansas in 1855. He came to the Willamette Valley in 1864, and after three years, moved to the Grande Ronde Valley. He settled two miles southeast of Joseph in 1872. Here he raised stock, operated a mill for eight years, and farmed. During the Bannock War of 1878, he was in the militia under Anderson C. Smith. James married **SARAH ANN REESE** in 1863. She was born on November 4, 1844. James died July 19, 1906 and Sarah on June 4, 1926. They are buried in the Alder Slope Cemetery near Enterprise.

EDWARD J. RENFROW was with the first settlers at Lost Prairie north of Flora. He was born on September 1, 1863 in Indiana. At 18 he moved to Iowa, then to Minnesota, and on to Yellowstone. He came to Baker City in 1882. He moved to Mud Flat in Wallowa County in 1883. His restless nature took him to Lost Prairie in the winter of 1884. He was among the first settlers there. He and his party used sleds to get to Lost Prairie. However, the snow was so deep that the sleds had to be abandoned at what became known as Sled Springs. He raised stock, grain, and fruit. He married **MARY A.**

WRIGHT at Cove in 1886. Ed died in 1936 and Mary in 1958. They are in the Enterprise Cemetery.

HENRY SCHAEFFER was another 1871 settler in Wallowa Valley. He was born in 1848 and died in 1927. He married **VIOLA POWERS,** daughter of Winslow P. Powers. She was born in 1855 and died in 1932. The Powers settled four miles north of Wallowa. Apparently, Henry's father, **SAMUEL SCHAEFFER,** lived with him. Samuel was born on February 20, 1802 and died on June 22, 1893. All of the Schaeffers are buried in the Bramlet Cemetery.

THOMAS ROUP was born on May 3, 1828 in New York. He moved to Iowa and farmed for 15 years. He proceeded to Montana to mine and run a hotel. He went back to Missouri and farmed for seven years. In 1874 he moved to six miles southwest of Joseph where he raised hay, grain, and hogs. He also built a sawmill. He became a justice of the peace in 1878. Tom married Nancy Henry in 1852. He died October 11, 1911 and is buried in the Prairie Creek Cemetery near Joseph.

JAMES J. STANLEY was born in Ohio on October 13, 1840. During the Civil War, he was a member of Company H, 20th Ohio Infantry. After the war, he moved to Iowa and taught school. He went to Colorado and then returned to Ohio to marry **MARY E. STROCK,** who was born on April 20, 1841. They moved to Iowa and then in 1869 to Colorado where he was a miner and carpenter. They moved to Joseph in 1881. He practiced carpentry and was justice of the peace from 1886-88. In 1897 he was mayor of Joseph. James died April 1, 1915 and Mary on December 29, 1926. They are buried in the Prairie Creek Cemetery.

WILLIAM KERNAN was born April 30, 1829 in Pennsylvania or Maryland. During the Civil War he was in Company K, 136th Pennsylvania Infantry and then later in Company G, 192nd Pennsylvania Infantry. He married Rachel Hockey in 1851, and after she died in 1856, William married Elizabeth Sipe in 1860. He moved to Kansas in 1877 and to Wallowa County southwest of Joseph in 1881. Here he raised sheep and farmed. William died January 4, 1903 and is buried in Joseph Cemetery.

DANIEL G. RALLS was born on February 18, 1851 in Missouri. He was trained as a blacksmith. He married **NORA (ELNORA** on tombstone) **PRATT** in 1870. She was born in 1853. They came to Joseph in 1884 where he practiced the blacksmith trade. In 1888 they moved northwest of Paradise— one of the first settlers in the area. He raised stock, ran a blacksmith shop, and operated a sawmill. Dan died on October 6, 1915 and Elnora in 1936. They are buried in the Paradise Cemetery.

LINCOLN AUSTIN was born September 21, 1859 or 1860 in Illinois. He moved to Kansas in 1879, to Colorado in 1881, and to Union County in 1884. He worked as a clerk in a store in Summerville. In 1886 he moved to Lost Prairie and homesteaded five miles northeast of present Flora. He was the second person in that area. He raised cattle and hogs. He bought a general merchandise store in Flora and was elected a deputy sheriff. He became a justice of the peace in 1890 and in 1898 a land commissioner. He died in 1922 and is buried in the Flora Cemetery.

RION H. BACON was born in October 1822 in New York. He went to California in 1849 and was responsible for erecting the first building in Sacramento. The family moved several times before coming to Baker City in 1882. Their son, Lorenzo Bacon, moved to Lost Prairie in 1884. Rion moved to Lost Prairie in 1885 to live with Lorenzo. The Bacons were one of the first homesteaders in the area. Rion died in 1906 and is buried in the Lost Prairie Cemetery.

THOMAS RICH was born in 1808. He and his wife **PRUDENCE (PRUDENA** on tombstone) were living in Massachusetts in 1838 and in Wisconsin 10 years later. They were in Oregon in 1860. They came to Wallowa County in 1883. Prudence was born in 1809 and died December 13, 1887. Tom died February 3, 1888. They are buried in the Enterprise Cemetery.

Their son, Thomas F. Rich was born on January 14, 1838 in Massachusetts. He came to Oregon in 1880 and ran a store at Prairie Creek east of Joseph. He had married **SARAH M. MARTIN** in Wisconsin in 1865. She was born April 30, 1839 in Pennsylvania. In 1884 or 1885 they moved to the Imnaha River and founded the hamlet of Fruita, which was named for Fruita, Colorado where they once lived. They were the first settlers in the area. They raised stock and had a large orchard. Sarah died November 8, 1913 and is buried in the Enterprise Cemetery.

WILLIAM M. McCORMACK was one of the first settlers in Wallowa County in 1871. He was born on July 29, 1841. His wife was **LUTHERIA McCORMACK**. She died on October 6, 1879, aged 20 years, 2 months, 7 days. William died on January 20, 1912. They are buried in the Alder Slope Cemetery, near Enterprise.

JACK W. JOHNSON was born in 1851. He was the first settler in the Imnaha area. He first came to Eagle Valley in the Richland area. Then in 1878 he settled at the mouth of Big Sheep Creek near the present site of the town of Imnaha. He was a scout for General O. O. Howard in the Bannock War. In 1884 he married **FLORENCE M. FINDLEY** who was born in 1860. She was the daughter of Mr. and Mrs. Alexander B. Findley who were with the first settlers in Wallowa County in 1872. Florence took the first homestead in the Findley Buttes area, which are named for her. Florence died in 1930 and Jack in 1931. They are buried in the Imnaha Cemetery.

MERTON WARNER BRUMBACH was born January 13, 1844. He and his family were the next homesteaders after Florence Findley in the Findley Buttes area in 1884. The largest of the Findley Buttes is Brumbach Butte, which is named for him. He died May 22, 1901 and is buried in the Joseph Cemetery.

Chapter 16
Malheur County Pioneers

Parts of southeastern Malheur County were settled earlier than much of the county because of the discovery of gold just across the border at Silver City and surrounding country. Supplies for the mines crossed the county in the Jordan Valley region. Stage lines also followed the same routes from California and Nevada.

JOHN R. (or E.) BAXTER was born May 3, 1835. (His tombstone claims 1834.) In 1864 he came with the first settlers to the Jordan Valley region. His home was at the present site of the town of Jordan Valley where he operated a stage station, a post office, and an inn. The place was originally called Baxterville, but the name was later changed to Jordan Valley. His wife was **ANNA E. BAXTER** who was born in Iowa in 1850. She married John in 1869. She died August 12, 1887 from a stomach tumor. John died September 10, 1887 from heart disease. They are buried in the Jordan Valley Cemetery.

ALEXANDER F. CANTER was born November 19, 1834. He arrived in Jordan Valley in 1864. He died July 29, 1910. He has an eight foot pillar in the Jordan Valley Cemetery.

JAMES E. GUSMAN was born February 23, 1835. By 1865 he was farming and ranching west of Jordan Valley. In 1871 he brought the first threshing machine to Jordan Valley from Winnemucca. His wife was **EMMA LOUISE GUSMAN**. She was born in 1852 and died in 1950. James died November 9, 1907. The Gusmans are buried in the Jordan Valley Cemetery.

The development of northern Malheur County was hastened in the 1860's by the discovery of gold in the Malheur City region. Two other factors likewise hastened this development. The presence of the Oregon Trail and the existence of the Dalles Military Road which extended from The Dalles to the Idaho border. This road passed through what is now Vale.

JOHN PEDERSON was born August 8, 1827 in Denmark. He became a sailor before moving to New York and then New Orleans. He went to Utah in 1858 and to California in 1860. He moved to Willow Creek in 1863, and then in 1865, he became the first settler on the Malheur River above Vale. He built an irrigation ditch for his farming. He died May 17 or 18, 1899. He is buried in the desolate Vale Pioneer Cemetery.

WILLIAM L. LOGAN was born May 31, 1827 in Tennessee. He moved to Illinois and Wisconsin before traveling by ox team to California to mine in 1852. He came to Walla Walla in 1862 and then moved on to the Idaho mines. He freighted from Umatilla to the mines. He married **NANCY JANE HARRIS** in 1863. She was from Illinois and came to the West by wagon train from Iowa. The Logans moved to the junction of the Snake and Weiser Rivers where they ran a stage station, farmed, and raised stock. They built the first house in Weiser, Idaho. In 1868 they moved to lower Willow Creek near Jamieson. In 1869 they again moved; this time to near Brogan to farm and raise stock. The Logan stone home is still standing. The Logans had eleven children. Nancy was born in 1848 and died in 1932. William died April 5, 1909. They are buried in the Jamieson (Dell) Cemetery.

Joshua L. Cole was born March 29, 1832 in Indiana. He married **MALINDA WISE** in 1856. She was born on July 8, 1837. They moved to Minnesota in 1858, to Boise in 1864, and to Malheur County in 1868. They settled on lower Willow Creek in 1872 to raise stock and care for 500 hives of bees. Malinda died June 18, 1896 and is buried in the Dell Cemetery at the south edge of Jamieson.

ROBERT A. LOCKETT was born November 29, 1838 in Kentucky. He moved to Missouri in 1858, and the next year he went to Pikes Peak to mine. He returned to Kentucky and during the Civil War was in Company A, 10 Ky Cavalry of Confederate Army where he became a first lieutenant. He crossed the plains to Salt Lake in 1865 and then moved on to Boise. In 1871 he arrived in Umatilla County where he married **MARY E. OWENS.** They moved to the mouth of the Owyhee River to raise stock in 1872. They next settled a mile north of Dell (present Jamieson) in 1879 where they raised hay and cattle. Robert was elected to the State Legislature where he dictated the bill that established Malheur County. He also was a justice of peace. Mary was born in 1856 and died in 1909. Robert died in 1920. They are buried in the Dell Cemetery.

WILLIAM K. (or S.) STARK was born September 3, 1819. His wife was **MARGARET STARK.** William came from Idaho City in 1871 to six miles south of Ontario to raise hay and cattle. He became the cattle king of the area. William died December 31, 1890. Margaret died on August 5, 1897, aged 61 years. They are buried in the Dell Cemetery.

WILLIAM S. GLENN was born March 14, 1815 in Ohio. He moved to Iowa and married **NANCY C. GLENN.** (Another source claims his wife was Mary Beckwith.) Nancy was born November 24, 1831. William led a wagon train from Iowa to the Grande Ronde Valley in 1862 where he took a claim near Summerville. In 1868 he moved to the Eldorado Mines and opened the first store in the town of Malheur City. In 1871, William moved to near Jamieson where he opened a store and was postmaster. He moved to Vale in 1887 and became its first mayor in 1889. William died May 7, 1900 and Nancy on April 15, 1909. They are buried in the Vale Pioneer Cemetery.

WILLIAM "BILLY" G. THOMPSON (THOMSON) was born December 6, 1849 in Arkansas. He came to the Willamette Valley by ox team in 1853 with his family. In 1866 he moved to Castle Rock and raised cattle. After attending Whitman College, he taught school in Pilot Rock in 1866 at 17 years of age. He moved to near Brogan in 1872 where his father, James, had arrived in 1871. William taught

the first school in the county in 1873 near Jamieson. His wife was **LYDIA ANN THOMPSON,** who was born in 1856. Three of their children died of diphtheria in less than a week. William was a scout for General O. O. Howard during the Bannock War of 1878. He was the first superintendent of schools in Malheur County. In 1904, he became Malheur County clerk. When he died in September 1939, he was the last of the scouts of the Bannock War. Lydia died in 1924. They are buried in the Dell Cemetery.

JOHN STEPHEN EDWARDS was born November 25, 1849 in Iowa. He came by ox team to Lane County with his parents in 1854. He arrived in Vale in 1871 as one of its first settlers. He moved to near Ontario in 1873 to raise stock. He married Sarah Smith of Union County in 1876. She was born on December 24, 1857. She was born in Iowa and came to Island City in 1864. John also owned mines in the Cornucopia area. Sarah died November 2, 1908 and John on December 12, 1915. They are buried in the Dell Cemetery.

FRANCIS "FRANK" O'NEILL was born May 10, 1846 in Ireland. (His tombstone claims the date as May 12, 1845.) He came to Pittsburgh in 1870 and on to California in 1871. He married **MARY MULLARY** in 1875. She was born March 20, 1847 and died March 23, 1883. They had moved to Portland in 1881 and then on to Willow Creek. Frank married Anna Jackson in 1886 and moved to the O'Neill Hot Springs on the Burns to Ontario pioneer road about 15 miles west of Vale. They had a stage station at the hot springs. Anna's first husband had been murdered at the hot springs. Frank died March 9, 1920 and is buried with his first wife, Mary, in the Dell Cemetery.

JOHN B. McLAUGHLIN was born January 13, 1827 in Missouri. He first moved to Kentucky before heading for California in 1848 and mined until 1861 when he proceeded to Walla Walla and then to Idaho. In 1863, he operated a ferry across the Snake River with Jonathan Keeney and John Du Vall. It was the first ferry at that part of the river. He sold the ferry in 1866. He married **BETHSINAH J. FROMAN (BETHSINA** on tombstone) in 1865. She was born in 1847. They moved to Willow

Creek in 1878, and in 1880, they settled on the south side of the Malheur River nine miles west of Vale. John died March 26, 1901 and his wife in 1926. They are buried in Vale's Valley View Cemetery.

MILTON G. HOPE was born August 31, 1859 in Wisconsin. He went to Kansas in 1870 and to California in 1880. He moved on to Idaho in 1882 and then to near Vale in 1883. He and his brother,

Isaiah, opened a store there in 1887. The store was robbed in 1895. Milton's wife was **EMMA H. HOPE** according to her tombstone, but another source says his wife was Sarah J. High. Emma was born September 28, 1862. Milton was a mayor of Vale, and for eight years, he was also its postmaster. Emma died December 20, 1904 and Milton in 1927. They are in Vale's Valley View Cemetery.

Chapter 17
Harney County Pioneers

Harney County had no gold rush, so the county was settled later than the Canyon City and Baker regions. The first settlers of Harney County were the cattlemen who came for the abundant grass. Three great "cattle barons" eventually owned much of the best land and water rights. They were John Devine, Peter French, and Henry Miller.

JOHN S. DEVINE was born November 10, 1839 in Virginia. He went to California and then in 1868 he went to the Whitehorse Ranch east of Steens Mountain. He rapidly expanded his cattle operation and soon owned the Alvord Ranch, Island Ranch, Mann Lake Ranch, Juniper Lake Ranch, and the Anderson Valley Ranch. At one time Devine owned 150,000 acres. Harsh winters and drought forced him into bankruptcy in 1889. Henry Miller took over the ranches but gave the Alvord Ranch back to John Devine. John led a regal life, wore elegant clothes, and entertained visitors in an elaborate manner. He also raised fine racing horses. Devine died on September 13, 1901. He has a large monument beside a tombstone in the Burns Cemetery.

JOHN CATLOW was born in England on November 5, 1824 (The metal marker at his grave gives the year as 1830.) He arrived in New York at the age of 16. He moved to Boston and then to California in 1861. He arrived at Silver City, Idaho in 1864. He became rich, apparently from mining gold and raising cattle. In 1872, he drove a herd of cattle to Harney County south of Fields in the Pueblo Valley. John had two ranches in this valley—one ranch was on Trout Creek and the other one at the base of Pueblo Mountain at Catlow Creek about ten miles north of Denio. He married **MARGARET FINN**, who was born in 1852 in England. She had a life-size painting of herself that cost $5,000! John died in 1901 and Margaret in 1925.

They are buried in their private cemetery about half a mile up Catlow Creek from their stone house. The cemetery is hidden in tall sagebrush. His grave is marked by a rock slab lying on the ground and a metal marker. Margaret's grave has a small pile of flat stones and a metal marker.

The Catlow stone house still stands and is being renovated. The original stone walls are three feet thick and the later walls are two feet thick. The stones were quarried a few miles from the house. Catlow Valley, west of Steens Mountain, is named for John Catlow although he never lived there.

PETER F. STENGER was born on October 16, 1852. In 1874 or '75, he left Douglas County and settled at the Sod House near Harney Lake. He established a horse ranch east of the site of Burns. He became a partner in George McGowan's store at Egan (now Hines). They moved the store to Burns in 1883. Peter had a beautiful wife who attracted Rush Frazier. At some point Peter shot and killed Frazier. Peter died on August 24, 1896 and is buried in the Burns Cemetery.

GEORGE McGOWAN was born in Scotland in 1845. He eventually settled in the Willamette Valley. In May 1882 he established a store at Egan (now Hines). The store was moved to Burns in 1883. George named the town after the Scottish poet, Robert Burns. George often is referred to as the founder of Burns. He became its postmaster in 1884. In 1886 he was elected Harney County Clerk. He married **MARY JANE MARTIN** in 1873. She was born in 1857 and died in 1928. George died in 1930. They share a large pink granite stone with a son and daughter in the Burns Cemetery.

ALPHENA VENATOR was born in 1863, the son of Jezreel (or Jezereal) and Elizabeth Venator. The family came to Harney County in 1873 and settled at Wrights Point. Here they raised cattle. They sold out to Peter Devine in 1877 and moved to near Lakeview. In 1884 Alphena and brother, **IRA K. VENATOR** move to the South Fork of the Malheur River. The former hamlet of Venator was named for them. Ira Venator was born in 1853. His wife was **JOSEPHINE G. VENATOR,** who was born in 1862. Alphena's wife was **LUELLA VENATOR,** who was born on May 14, 1873 and died November 11, 1899. Ira died in 1937, Alphena in 1951, and Josephine in 1931. The Venators are buried in the Burns Cemetery.

WILLIAM CARROLL CECIL was born in 1847. He and his brother, Logan, in 1871, established a horse ranch. It was named the 71 Bar Ranch, and was located at the site of Camp Currey. Camp Currey was a military establishment built in 1865 and abandoned in 1866. It was located on Silver Creek northwest of Riley. The Cecil brothers later raised cattle. The ranch was in the family for over 100 years, and more recently, it has been known as the Mayo Ranch. Carl Mayo married the granddaughter of Carroll. Carroll Cecil's wife was **NANNIE OLIVE CECIL,** who was born in 1864 and died in 1959. Carroll died in 1930. They are buried in the Burns Cemetery.

THOMAS JEFFERSON SHIELDS was born in Missouri on August 17, 1849. He arrived in Linn County in 1852. He was in Douglas County in 1865 but then moved back to Linn County. In 1871 he moved to northern California and built the first house in Alturas. He was a teacher. He moved to Lakeview where he married **JULIA A. GARRETT** in 1880. She was born October 11, 1861. They moved to Silver Creek two miles northwest of Riley in 1884 to raise cattle and run a dairy. He was the first judge of Harney County. Thomas died on January 7, 1943 and Julia on June 8, 1951. They are buried in the Silver Creek Cemetery near Suntex.

ROBERT J. BAKER settled on Silver Creek four miles southeast of Camp Currey in 1876. He fought in the battle at Silver Creek during the Bannock War on June 23, 1878. One account states that his wife died at Fort Harney in 1878. However, in the Silver Creek Cemetery, there is a sheet metal marker beside Robert's marker that states **LORETTA BAKER** died in 1885. Was Loretta his second wife? Robert died in 1891. His grave is marked by a sheet metal marker and a small stone inscribed RJB.

Chapter 18
Crook County Pioneers

DAVID WAYNE CLAYPOOL, WILLIAM SMITH and several others came to Central Oregon to live in 1867. They settled near the mouth of Mill Creek about nine miles east of the present city of Prineville. Indians destroyed everything they had, so they had to return to the Willamette Valley, but they returned in 1868 with their families. They were the first settlers in that part of Central Oregon. Wayne Claypool was born in Indiana on October 8, 1834. He crossed the plains to Lebanon with his folks. He fought in the Yakima Indian War of 1856. He married LOUISA ELKINS in 1857. She was born February 1, 1835. She died on August 16, 1892, and Wayne died January 30, 1899. They are buried in the Mill Creek Cemetery east of Prineville.

William Smith was a native of England. He died on February 27, 1914 at 85 years of age. He is also buried in the Mill Creek Cemetery.

SILAS E. HODGES was born in 1859 and died in 1930. He came to Prineville in 1869 with his parents, the Alexander Hodges. Silas operated the Grindstone Ranch near Paulina by 1879. He returned to Prineville in 1895 and operated a livery stable. He married SUSANNAH THOMPSON HEARING. She died on January 31, 1908 at the age of 54 years, 1 month, and 21 days. They are buried in the Prineville Cemetery.

ALEXANDER HODGES was born on August 28, 1823 according to the inscription on his tombstone. One writer claims he was born in 1835 in Indiana. He moved to Missouri and then to Albany, Oregon in 1846. He was married twice. He married his second wife Dulcina Tomlinson in 1853. He moved to Prineville in 1869. In 1870 he located his family and his brother, Monroe Hodges, in Prineville. The Hodges raised stock. Alexander died from pneumonia on March 2, 1891. After his death, Dulcina moved to Dufur to live with her daughter, Mrs. Jacob Gulliford.

MONROE HODGES lived from 1833 to 1905. He came to Oregon in 1846 or '47. His wife was RHODA HODGES, who was born March 5, 1838. Her mother was SARAH WILSON JOHNSON (1816-1880). In 1870, the young rancher, Monroe, bought out Barney Prine at the future site of Prineville for a horse and twenty dollars. Monroe built the first hotel in Prineville. He also established the first livery stable and the first meat market in the town. He raised many horses on his ranch. Rhoda died on July 11, 1898. Monroe, Rhoda, and Sarah are all buried in the Prineville Cemetery.

COL. MICHAEL C. NYE died July 13, 1906 and is buried in the Prineville Cemetery. He refused to tell when he was born, but it is believed that his birth was in the early 1820's in Virginia. He moved to Missouri, and in 1841 he joined up with the John Bidwell party to travel to California as its youngest member. The Bidwell-Bartleson party was the first wagon train to California. The Spanish and Mexicans in California were quarreling and revolting, so the Mexican government sent General Manuel Micheltorena to take over in 1842. Nye joined the general as a soldier, and as a result he became a Mexican citizen and was given a land grant. However, he switched sides and volunteered to fight in the Bear Flag War under Colonel John C. Fremont in 1846. It is claimed that he was one of the rescuers of the Donner Party of 1846 after winter blocked the party at the east base of the Sierra Mountains. Many in the Donner Party died of starvation and there was extensive cannibalism. Later, Nye married one of the survivors in 1847. His wife was either Harriet Pike or Harriet Wright. Nye was a friend of Sutter and made a fortune, apparently from gold mining, but lost most of it. He moved to

The Dalles in 1864 and raised cattle. Harriet died there or in California in 1870. In 1878 or '79, he came to the Prineville area and became a very prosperous sheep raiser and a large land owner.

WILLIAM ADAMS was born on October 24, 1838 in Missouri. He moved to Colorado in 1859 and on to the Idaho mines. He later came to Lane County. He married **NANCY A. MAUPIN** in 1867. She was born on February 18, 1850. In 1871 they moved to Beaver Creek in the Paulina area. Later they lived at Combs Flat where they raised sheep. They also had a home in Prineville. Nancy died September 20, 1901 and William on April 27, 1913. They lie in the Prineville Cemetery.

WILLIAM ROBERT McFARLAND was born in Missouri in 1844. He was a veteran of the Civil War. He came to Sheridan, Oregon in 1871 where he taught school. He married **LUCY JANE MASTERSON** in 1874. She was born in 1857. They moved to John Day in 1880 and then to the Prineville area. He taught in Prineville and became county surveyor in 1884. He became Crook County school superintendent in 1894. Lucy died in 1919 and William in 1927. They are buried in the Prineville Cemetery.

DAVID TEMPLETON was born on May 4, 1831 in Indiana. He moved to Missouri in 1837. He came from Missouri to Linn County in 1847 or 1852. He married **LAVINA PELL**, who was born in 1835 and who came to Oregon in 1852 from Ohio. Dave had struck gold in California in 1849. They moved to McKay Creek near Prineville in 1870 and raised cattle. He also ran a drug store. Dave died December 28, 1908 and Lavina in 1914. Their tombstones in Prineville are horizontal cylinders beside a large Templeton monument.

JACKSON J. VANDEVERT was born in 1824. He came from New York to Cottage Grove in the early 1840's. He married Grace Clark, a survivor of the Raft River Massacre. She died in 1874. Then Jackson and his sons, Walter and Charles, moved to the north slope of Powell Butte. Jackson died in 1906 and is buried in the Prineville Cemetery.

GEORGE McINTIRE (MACK) CORNETT was born October 21, 1859 in Virginia. He moved to Kentucky and then to Central Oregon in 1881. He started a stage coach business with over 500 miles of route with 360 horses and over 100 stage coaches. In 1910 he began using cars as stages. He opened a store in addition in 1907 and also raised sheep. He was a deputy sheriff for a time. He married **EFFIE BLANCH TONEY** in 1893. She was the daughter of the Toneys of Girds Creek near Richmond. She was born in 1867 and died in 1917. Mack died in 1932. They are buried in the Prineville Cemetery.

TILLMAN H. GLAZE was born in 1843. He came with his parents to Dallas in Polk County when he was 9 years of age. He moved to Prineville in 1878 and bought a saloon. He had to leave Polk County because he had shot and killed a father and son in self-defense. He organized the first musical band in Central Oregon. He also had a livery stable in Prineville and raced horses around the State. Till's wife, **ANNE E. GLAZE**, was born in 1843. They had four children. Daughter, **MARGARET**, was born in 1869. A photographer, W. B. Flowers, was in love with Margaret, but she refused to marry him. Mr. Flower always superimposed Margaret's photo on his commercial photographs. Till was killed in a gun fight by Bud Howard in Burns, apparently over some quarrel involving Till's race horse, Wasco, in 1894. Bud Howard also was killed in the fight. Anne died in 1939, Margaret in 1944, and son **WARREN** (1880-1973). All are buried in the pioneer section of the Prineville Cemetery.

MICHAEL CHRISTIANI was born in Europe in 1831. He came to New York when he was 22. He moved to Wisconsin and then to Colorado to mine. He later mined in Idaho and then in Montana in 1862. Gold lured him to British Columbia in 1864. He moved to Portland and finally to Prineville in 1873 where he raised sheep. He married Malinda Jane Barnard in 1882. She had been born in Linn County on February 6, 1866. Michael died in 1909 and is buried in the Prineville Cemetery.

An interesting story is told about Michael Christiani during his bachelor days at Prineville. He could not find a wife, so when Sam Newsom traveled to Kentucky on a horse deal, he asked Sam to look for a wife for him. Michael promised to pay Sam's expenses for looking for a wife. Sam hired a buggy for $2.50 to see a widow, but she refused to move West to marry Michael. When Sam returned to Prineville, Michael refused to pay the $2.50 since Sam had not returned with a wife. Sam went to court and collected his $2.50. In addition, Michael had to pay $1.50 in court charges.

FULGENZIO VANINA was a world traveler. He was born in Switzerland on July 15, 1844. He shipped to Australia in 1856 and mined all over Australia and New Zealand. He returned to Switzerland in 1872. He traveled to California and Nevada. In 1882 he journeyed to The Dalles to ranch. Then, in 1884 he came to the Prineville area and raised cattle. He became one of the wealthiest settlers in the region. He married **CATHERINA (CATARINA) RIVERA** in 1878. She was born in Switzerland in 1852. She had moved to California in 1877. Fulgenzio died on August 21, 1916 and Catherina in 1924. They are buried in the Prineville Cemetery.

WILLIAM WIGLE was born in 1835 and died in 1913. He married **MARTHA J. SPALDING**, daughter of the missionary H. H. Spalding. She was born March 20, 1845 at the Lapwai Mission near Lewiston, Idaho. She was educated at Forest Grove and then moved to Walla Walla. After she married William in 1859, they moved to eastern Oregon to raise stock. They settled in the Prineville area in 1886. Martha died in 1924. The Wigles are buried in the Prineville Cemetery.

JEROME B. LAFOLLETTE (LAFOLLETT on tombstone) was born August 17, 1831 in Indiana. He married **SOPHIA J. HOWARD**, who was born on May 16, 1831, in Tennessee. They moved to Iowa and then to near Salem in 1862. They proceeded to Linn County in 1865. They were among the first settlers in the Prineville area in 1871. About 1876 they moved to Camp Creek and raised stock. They moved again to McKay Creek north of Prineville in 1881 and raised horses. Jerome also ran a blacksmith shop and livery stable in Prineville. Jerome was accidently killed while haying on November 6, 1884. Sophia died on January 6, 1912. They are buried in the Prineville Cemetery.

ANDREW LYTLE was born August 11, 1833 in Ohio. He traveled to California at the age of 17. He transferred to Canyon City as a blacksmith and also operated a freight outfit from The Dalles. He

moved to Salem and married Sarah Lodema Ramp in 1868. They then settled at the southeast side of Grizzly Mountain in the 1870's. Lytle Creek, northwest of Prineville, is named for them. Andrew died on April 26, 1895 and lies in the Lytle plot in the Prineville Cemetery.

WALLACE POST and brother, **WILLIAM H. POST**, were the founders of the hamlet of Post. Wallace was born November 19, 1847 in Illinois. He moved to Missouri and then to California. He arrived in Polk County in 1859 and in Benton County in 1864. He married **LUCY E. HERBERT** in 1866. She was born in Benton County on July 23, 1851. The Posts all moved to the Post area in 1885 or 1886 to raise sheep and later cattle. William Post died April 21, 1919 and Wallace on November 12, 1919. Lucy died August 5, 1921. The Posts are buried in the Prineville Cemetery.

WILLIAM G. O'NEIL was born September 6, 1812 in Tennessee. He moved to Indiana, Kansas, and California before arriving in Crook County in 1881. He ran a store 13 miles west of Prineville at O'Neil. The store was at the junction of the pioneer Willamette Valley and Cascade Mountain Military Road and the Huntington Road. His wife was **ELECTA O'NEIL** who was born in Massachusetts in 1825. William died December 5, 1897 and Electa in 1903. They are in the Prineville Cemetery. They are buried with **RACEL (RACHEL) O'NEIL**, who may have been their daughter.

WILLIAM ADAMS was born October 24, 1838 in Missouri. He moved to Colorado in 1859 and on to the Idaho mines. He then came to Lane County. He married **NANCY A. MAUPIN** in 1867. In 1871, they became some of the first settlers on Beaver Creek in the Paulina area. Later, they moved to Combs Flat southeast of Prineville where they raised sheep. They also had a home in Prineville. Nancy was born February 8, 1850 and died September 20, 1901. William died April 27, 1913. They are buried in the Prineville Cemetery.

JAMES PARKER COMBS was born August 10, 1822 in Ohio. He married **JANE DYER** in 1847 in Illinois. She was born March 19, 1827. They had ten children. In 1847 they crossed the plains to near Lebanon. They moved to Ochoco Creek in the

Prineville area in 1870 where they farmed. Their land extended to Combs Flat, which is named for them. James died April 1, 1900 and Jane on January 7, 1913. They are buried in the Prineville Cemetery.

JOHN HENRY GRAY was born April 23, 1855 in Linn County. He married **REBECCA ANN HUNSAKER** in 1875. They moved to the Prineville area in 1876 and settled on Combs Flat. They sold out in 1899 and moved 24 miles southeast of Prineville to start the famous Bonny View (Bonnieview) Ranch, which still exists. Here they raised cattle. John was county assessor in 1894 and sheriff in 1896. John died in 1928 and Rebecca in 1935. Their graves are in the Prineville Cemetery.

JOHN BENJAMIN SHIPP was born in England in 1858. He came to Canada and then the United States. He was awarded the contract for the first school house on the Warm Springs Reservation in the 1890's. He built the historic Charles Elkin house in Prineville in 1897. Over the years, he built many other homes in Prineville as well as two churches. His greatest construction job was building the Crook County Courthouse in 1908. He also ran a bicycle shop. John died in 1942 and is buried in the Prineville Cemetery.

JOHN NEWTON WILLIAMSON was born on November 5, 1855 in Lane County. He married **SARAH V. FORREST** in 1882. They came to Powell Butte and later to Prineville. Newton had a large sheep ranch and also published a Prineville newspaper. He was very active in politics being a member of the State Legislature, Speaker of the House, State Senator, and US Congressman. He was the county sheriff and helped put an end to the Vigilantes. For many years, he was the Prineville postmaster before retiring to farm on Ochoco Creek. Newton died in November 1943 and Sarah in December, 1949. They are buried in the Prineville Cemetery.

DR. HORACE P. BELKNAP was born in Benton County in 1856. He came to Crook County with his parents in 1875 and raised stock. He was educated at the University of Michigan where he received his medical degree in 1886. He returned to Prineville and became a famous doctor. He married **ALWILDA "WILDA" KETCHUM** in 1888. He was elected county school superintendent in 1892 and county treasurer in 1894. He was mayor of Prineville for several years. His fame spread when he discovered that Rocky Mountain spotted fever was caused by the bite of an infected tick in 1899. All during this time, he traveled many miles to treat sick or injured patients. Dr. Belknap died in 1936 and Wilda in 1957. They are buried in the Prineville Cemetery.

JULIUS S. McCOIN was born November 8, 1850 in North Carolina. He moved to Kansas where he married **SARAH F. OSBORN**. They traveled to California in 1877 and later to Goose Lake in the Lakeview area where he freighted between Red Bluff, California and Lakeview. They proceeded to McKay Creek near Prineville in 1882. In 1886 they moved to the Haystack Butte area where Julius freighted between The Dalles and Prineville. Sarah died in 1888. Julius outlived her by 40 years when he died in 1928. They share a tombstone in the Prineville Cemetery.

JOHN MARTIN ZEVELY was born in Missouri in 1822. He crossed the plains to Scio in 1853. Later he settled at Cove in Union County and raised fruit. John moved to upper Ochoco Creek in 1886 and raised stock. He married Hannah Barilla Walker, but she left him. Apparently, he married again as he shares a tombstone with **M. A. ZEVELY**, age 68 years—no dates. John died November 24, 1899, aged 77 years. The Zevelys are buried in the Howard Cemetery about two miles beyond the abandoned Howard School.

JAMES H. SNODERLY was born March 17, 1830. He married **ELIZA CURL** in 1855. She was born April 3, 1837 in Missouri. She took the Oregon Trail to Linn County in 1853. The Snoderlys moved to the Ochoco near Prineville in 1869. James died May 14, 1898 and Eliza on February 18, 1922. They are buried in the Prineville Cemetery.

GEORGE M. STANCLIFT (STANCLIFF) was born in 1835 in New York and died on March 18, 1913. His wife was **MARY C. (HILL) STANCLIFT** who was born in 1832. She crossed the plains on horseback to California and then to Oregon. They were married in 1867. The Stanclifts lived in the

Prineville area. Mary died in December 1915. They are buried in the Prineville Cemetery.

JOHN W. HOUSTON was born in North Carolina in 1834. His wife was **JULETTA M. HOUSTON.** Their children had moved to Crook County at an early age. In their old age, the Houstons moved to be with their children. John died on August 3, 1919 after an operation for a tumor. Juletta died in 1925. They are in the Prineville Cemetery.

DAVID PRINE was born on January 2, 1831 in Missouri. He worked for the government during the Mexican War. During his youth he was a frontiersman. He married **ELIZABETH REY** in 1850. Elizabeth was born in 1830. They moved to Linn County in 1852. In 1872 the Prines became early settlers of Crook County. Dave was the nephew of Barney Prine for whom Prineville is named. David's obituary states he died on May 29, 1890, but the date on his tombstone is May 30. Elizabeth died in 1904. The Prines are buried in different parts of the Prineville Cemetery.

STOWELL CRAM was one of the first people killed by an airplane in the United States! He was born in 1831. The Crams were early pioneers of Crook County. In October 1912 he was struck by a Curtiss biplane and died. He has an elaborate dark tombstone in the Prineville Cemetery.

THOMAS JEFFERSON LOGAN was born August 6, 1826. In 1862 he left Iowa for the Portland area. Soon, he drove horses and mules to Umatilla Landing and sold them to a stage company. For a year, Tom ran a stage station in the Hermiston area. He bought a ranch near Corvallis and ran it until 1869. In 1870 the Logan family brought cattle to south of Prineville. The Logans were the first to run cattle in the Bear Creek and Camp Creek area. Logan Butte, famous for its fossils, is named for the family. Tom died July 10, 1894 and has a very elaborate monument in the Prineville Cemetery.

Chapter 19
Jefferson County Pioneers

Parts of what later became Jefferson County were settled at an early date. These areas include parts of Trout Creek and the Grizzly region. Other parts of the county such as the Agency Plains and much of the Madras area only became settled after dry land farming became popular around the turn of the century.

PERRY CRAM was born September 5, 1829. He graduated from Dartmouth College and went to California by ship to mine. He was a friend of General Bidwell and later named a son after the general. In 1859, he returned to New Hampshire and married Mary Ann Scully. They had eleven children. They moved to Texas to raise stock but were forced to move because they were Unionists during the Civil War. They came to California by way of Mexico. The Crams came to Oregon and took charge of the toll station in Cow Canyon in 1880 on the road between Madras and Shaniko. Perry died on May 27, 1909 and is buried in the Prineville Cemetery where he has a striking seven foot monument.

EDWARD GABRIEL BOLTER was born on Prince Edward Island, Canada on September 12, 1830. He moved to Springfield, Massachusetts and became a cabinet maker. He went around the Horn to get to the Willamette Valley. In 1859 he married **ELIZABETH MATILDA MAY.** She was born on January 10, 1841 and had crossed the plains from Missouri to California in 1848. She arrived in Salem in 1852. Ed ran stores in Portland and Dallas before coming to Prineville in 1876. In 1878 the Bolters homesteaded on Trout Creek. Their home was finished in 1879, and Ed's skill as a cabinet builder still shows in the home of his grandson. The Bolters kept travelers at their stage stop along the pioneer road that ran by their house. They operated the Cross Keys Post Office from 1879. Ed died July

12, 1906 and Elizabeth (Bettie to her friends) on May 11, 1914. They are buried in the Hay Creek Cemetery.

THOMAS SHARP HAMILTON was born March 10, 1850 in Missouri. He crossed the plains with his parents in 1853 to south of Eugene. He moved to Lake County in 1870 and then on to Reno, Nevada to herd sheep. He moved to Summer Lake in Lake County in 1873. At first he raised cattle but soon switched to sheep. In 1878, he moved to Trout Creek south of Ashwood. He was one of the first settlers on Trout Creek and was the first to bring shorthorn cattle to the area. Later he ran sheep also. By about 1900 he owned 2840 acres, 7500 sheep, and 200 cattle. He married **PHOEBE LORENDA CROOKS** in 1889. She was born in 1859 and died in 1936. Tom died in 1929. Tom's parents, **ANDERSON HAMILTON** and **ELIZABETH HAMILTON,** were also in the area. Anderson was born on October 11, 1821 and died March 27, 1900. Elizabeth was born on April 6, 1824 and died December 31, 1877. All the Hamiltons are buried in the Prineville Cemetery.

Phoebe's father, Aaron H. Crooks, and her first husband, Stephen J. Jory, were murdered in 1882 by Lucius Langdon over a boundary dispute. Even relatives of Crooks and Jory do not know where they are buried!

COLUMBUS FRIEND was born on May 23, 1845 in Iowa. He moved to the Willamette Valley in 1870 and then to near Ashwood on Trout Creek. Here he raised cattle and later sheep. In 1888 he married **HENRIETTA "NETTIE" (CROOKS) BROWN HALE.** She was born August 14, 1863 in Linn County. She was another daughter of Aaron Crooks. She married John Brown, who deserted her. Henrietta then married Daniel Hale. Columbus met her while she was driving a freight wagon in order to support her children from these previous marriages. Columbus died November 1, 1901 and Henrietta on October 11, 1930. They are buried in the Maupin Cemetery near Ashwood.

JAMES M. GRATER was born March 10, 1822. He was the first permanent settler near Ashwood when he arrived in 1871 or 1872. He had come from Iowa. He first raised cattle but shifted to sheep. He married **MARTHA FRIEND** in 1880. She was the mother of Columbus Friend, but after her husband died, she married James. She was born on April 30, 1822 and died March 19, 1887. James died May 31, 1903. They are buried in the Maupin (sometimes called Friend) Cemetery near Ashwood. She is buried inside the iron fence of the Friend plot, but he is just outside the fence next to her. Some of the Friend family disliked James, so when they built the fence, they left James outside! James' tombstone is broken and now lies on the ground.

KNOX HUSTON and **VICTORIA (KNOX) HUSTON** became early settlers of upper Trout Creek when they drove a band of sheep over the Cascade Mountains to the Ashwood area in 1878. He was born March 10, 1839 and she on December 9, 1839. In 1890 he was elected surveyor of Crook County, and they moved to Prineville. Knox died on April 10, 1906 and Victoria on April 23, 1917. They are buried in the Prineville Cemetery.

PERRY READ was born May 11, 1849 in Benton County near Corvallis. In 1871 he became one of the first settlers on upper Willow Creek in the Grizzly area. He married **HATTIE ELLEN MONTGOMERY** in 1873. She had moved to the area in 1872 with her father, Kennedy Montgomery. She was born on May 15, 1856 in Brownsville. The Reads did some farming and raised horses. They hired Indians to herd the horses. They moved to near Culver in 1895 or 1897 and ran a hotel. Perry died in 1932 and Hattie in 1950. They are in the Madras Cemetery.

NANNIE A. (MAYES) HOLT was the first person buried in the Madras Cemetery. She had homesteaded the area where the cemetery is located. When she knew she was dying, she showed her father where she wanted to be buried. She came from Tennessee. She was born September 19, 1865

and died September 21, 1901 or 1904. She is buried by her folks, **JAMES D. MAYES** and **SARAH E. MAYES**. James was born October 31, 1838 and died May 22, 1936. Sarah was born February 5, 1838 and died December 27, 1916.

ANDREW MORROW was born in Ireland in 1858. He moved to Wisconsin and then to California in 1883. There he helped to establish a paper mill. He came to Willow Creek in 1884 and went into partnership with James S. McMean. The ranch eventually became the famous Morrow-Keenan Ranch near Grizzly. During the cattle-sheep trouble of 1904, vigilantes killed a thousand of the Morrow-Keenan sheep. The ranch had thousands of sheep, several hundred cattle, and 6000 acres of dry land grain farming. Andrew married **EMILY GREENWALD** in 1911. She was born in 1877 in Michigan. In 1909 she came to Lamonta to teach and to homestead. She lived to be 103 years old. She died in 1980 and Andrew in 1948. They are buried in the Madras Cemetery.

JAMES S. McMEEN (or McMEAN) was Andrew Morrow's partner on what became the Morrow-Keenan Ranch in the Grizzly area. He was born on February 25, 1852 and died December 11, 1911. He is buried in the Gray Butte Cemetery between Prineville and Madras.

Several members of the Barnett family were early settlers in the Haystack Butte-Lamonta area. **ELIJAH M. BARNETT** was born March 14, 1826 in Ireland. The family lived in Iowa and then Missouri. They came to The Dalles and then to the Haystack Butte region in 1882. His wife was **ELEANOR F. BARNETT,** who was born on May 15, 1829. Elijah started the Haystack post office in 1890. Elijah died April 11, 1904 and Eleanor on November 9, 1918.

Elijah Barnett's brother, **ROBERT H. BARNETT,** was born in 1832 and died in 1923. Robert came to Albany in 1852. He moved to the Haystack Butte area with Elijah. For many years, he was an invalid. All the Barnetts are buried in the Gray Butte Cemetery.

SAMUEL RUSH was born April 24, 1829 in Alabama. His grandfather was the brother of Benjamin Rush, who was a signer of the Declaration of Independence. (One source says he was the grand-

Malheur County Pioneers

William Stark

William & Nancy Glenn

William Logan

Francis O'Neill

John Pederson

Robert A. & Mary Lockett

William G. Thompson

John Stephen Edwards

Harney County Pioneers

John Catlow

Mrs. John Catlow

Aaron Denio

George McGowen

Crook County Pioneers

David Wayne Claypool

Tillman and Ann Glaze

Monroe Hodges

Col. Micheal C. Nye

William O'Neil

David Prine

Jefferson County Pioneers

Bessie D. Thompson

Edward G. Bolter

Elijah M. Barnett

Samuel and Mary Rush

Perry Cram

Liborius Weigand

Deschutes County
Pioneers

Princess Gertrude Munz

PIONEER MAILMAN

On the knoll behind this sign once stood a
rustic cabin in which pioneer mailman
John Templeton Craig died in December, 1877. Craig,
who was 56, had been employed to carry the mail
between McKenzie Bridge and Camp Polk, near Sisters. While
carrying the christmas mail, Craig was caught in a sudden
storm and later found frozen to death inside the cabin by
a search party

McKENZIE PASS
SCENIC TOUR

John Templeton Craig

John Templeton Craig

Klamath County Pioneers

Winema

Lee and Joe Laws

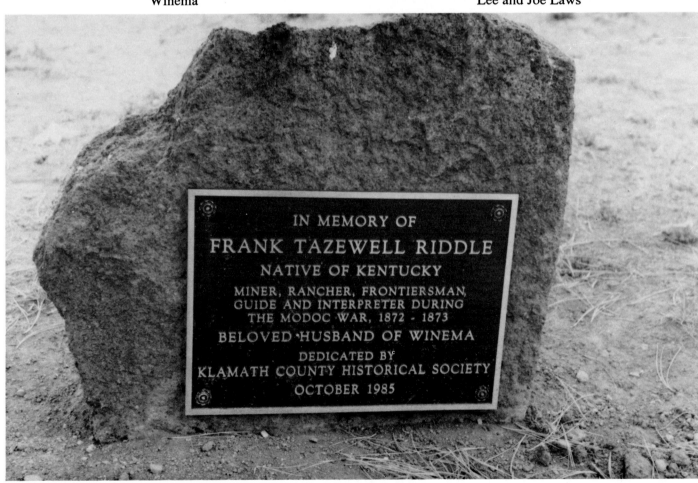

Frank Tazewell Riddle

Lake County Pioneers

James Foster

John Allen Withers

Thomas Jefferson Brattain

Dr. Bernard Daly

son of Benjamin Rush.) Sam moved to Arkansas in 1846. He took the Oregon Trail in 1853 to Oregon City and then to Eugene in 1853. His father, who was captain of the wagon train, died on the way. Only 45 of the 105 in the wagon train lived to reach Oregon! Sam married **MARY ELIZABETH BREEDING** in 1857. She was born December 25, 1838 in Missouri. The Rushes went to Jackson County in 1867 and then to the Lamonta area in 1884. Sam and Mary both died in 1926. They are buried in the Gray Butte Cemetery.

JOHN CARSON RUSH was born on August 27, 1861 in Eugene. His parents were Samuel and Mary Rush. In 1884 he homesteaded in the Lamonta area between Prineville and Madras with his parents. In 1905, he platted the town of Lamonta and operated a large general store there. John never married. It is said that his mother chased away all of his girl friends. John died in 1941 and is buried in Gray Butte Cemetery near his parents.

WHITFIELD T. WOOD was born December 29, 1830 in Illinois. He moved to Nebraska to farm. He also freighted from Omaha to Denver. He moved to California in 1863 and farmed until 1872 when he moved to the Willamette Valley. In 1880 he moved to the future site of Ashwood, where he raised cattle and sheep. He helped in the opening of various Ashwood area mines. He married **MARTHA J. RUSH** in 1861, in Nebraska. She was born in Ohio on October 27, 1847. Whitfield did not like Howard Maupin, so instead of being buried in Maupin's Cemetery, Whitfield started the Ashwood Cemetery. He died in 1923 and Martha in 1934.

JAMES WOOD was the son of Whitfield and Martha Wood. He was born on May 22, 1862 in Nebraska (The date is 1861 on his tombstone.) In 1880 he drove stock to the East. He came to Ashwood with his parents and raised stock. In 1899, he laid out the town of Ashwood and became its postmaster. He owned the Red Jacket Mine and was associated with the Oregon King Mine. James married **ADA BELLE RUSH** in 1902. She was born in 1873, the daughter of Samuel and Mary Rush. She died in 1922, and James died in 1937. They are buried in the Gray Butte Cemetery.

The Weigand family was early settlers in the Lamonta area. **LIBORIUS WEIGAND** has the earliest birth date. He was born July 25, 1825 and died May 4, 1910. He has an unusual dark, round, horizontal cylinder as a tombstone in the Gray Butte Cemetery.

JAMES HENRY WINDOM was born in 1857 in California. He married **REBECCA LEACH** in 1885. She was born in Brownsville in 1864. They moved to the Haystack area where he was the first to till the soil. He brought in the first horse-powered threshing machine. It was carried by wagon over the pioneer Santiam Pass Road. He also was involved in putting in the first pump to get water from Opal Spring to the plateau above about 1898. James died in 1913 and Rebecca in 1939. They are buried in the Gray Butte Cemetery.

JOHN EDWARD CAMPBELL was born in Oregon on November 14, 1865. In 1872 he moved to near Prineville with his father. He married **SARAH A. RODMAN** in 1885. She was born October 16, 1865 in California. They lived near Grizzly Mountain for ten years. In 1895, he bought the ferry on the Deschutes River near the Warm Springs bridge on Highway US 26. They ran the ferry until 1905. Ed carried the mail from The Dalles to Prineville by way of Wapinitia and Warm Springs from 1896 to 1902. In 1901 they homesteaded near the ferry at the mouth of a canyon. The Campbells had 11 children, so they built a school and hired a teacher for $35 a month. Ed died in 1917 and Sarah in 1946. They are buried in the Milo Gard Cemetery a few miles west of Madras.

The Agency Plains were first homesteaded in 1902. However, the area had been used for many years earlier by stockmen. A late snowstorm in the spring of 1885 killed 3000 sheep on the Agency Plains from starvation and the cold. **MILO O. GARD** was one of these 1902 homesteaders. Previously he had been a state representative from Clackamas County. Milo was born in 1844 and his wife, **CAROLINE GARD**, was born in 1855. She died in 1903, and her husband donated the land for the Milo Gard Cemetery. Milo died in 1907.

WILLIAM H. RAMSEY and his wife, **CLARA H. RAMSEY**, were other 1902 homesteaders of the

Agency Plains. He was born in 1851 and she in 1869. His family was from Missouri. They had the first child born on Agency Plains. William died in 1934 and Clara in 1948. They are buried in the Madras Cemetery.

CHARLES COOPER MALING (often misspelled Mailing) was born in England in 1837 and died in 1902. In 1877 he established the first sawmill in Jefferson County on upper Willow Creek near Grizzly Mountain. He is buried in the Prineville Cemetery.

Chapter 20

Deschutes County Pioneers

Settlers moved into the Bend and LaPine areas by the early 1880's. However, much of what became Deschutes County was not settled until after 1900. The first homesteaders arrived in the Redmond area about 1905 when water became available for irrigation. The High Desert region east of Bend was settled about the same time by dry land farmers. Thus, the white man's history in most of Deschutes County is very short. The county was not established until 1916.

One of the first settlers in the Bend area was **WILLIAM H. STAATS** from Monmouth. He was born in 1861. William's father visited Prineville to buy cattle and while there joined the vigilantes. He was killed while riding on Powell Butte. William visited the Bend area about 1880 and moved to the site of Bend in 1881. He married **EMMA A. TURPIN** in 1883. She was born on November 19, 1864 at Cottage Grove. The Staats ran a ranch, a store and an inn. William died in 1931 and Emma in 1949. They are buried in Bend's Pioneer Cemetery.

JOSHUA JACKSON VANDEVORT (JACKSON J. VANDEVERT on tombstone) was born in 1824 in Ohio. He arrived in the Willamette Valley in the 1840's. He married Grace Clark in 1853. In 1851 her family started for Oregon but they were killed in the Clark Massacre along the Snake River. Grace was partly scalped and left for dead. In 1874 Jackson homesteaded on the north slope of Powell Butte. He died in 1906 and is buried in the Prineville Cemetery.

WILLIAM PLUTARCH VANDEVERT was the son of Jackson and Grace Vandevert. He was born on February 24, 1854 in Cottage Grove. When he was 17, he helped drive cattle to California. Later he went to Texas where he met **SADIE LEE VINCEN-THELLER**. They were married in Kentucky in 1880. After working on the Hash Knife Outfit in

Texas, they moved to New York. They then moved to Powell Butte where William's father lived. In 1892 they moved to the Little Deschutes River, south of Sunriver, where they raised cattle. The ranch has remained in the family. Sadie died in 1924 and William in 1944. They are buried in the Bend Pioneer Cemetery.

FRANK T. REDMOND was the first settler in the Redmond area and gave the town its name. He was born in 1859. His wife was **JOSEPHINE D. RED-MOND**, who was born in 1865. They were married in 1896. He taught school in North Dakota before moving to Oregon in 1901. He taught school in Wasco and then moved to the site of future Redmond in 1904. He bought the first land sold by the Central Oregon Irrigation Company. In 1910 Frank left the farm and entered the real estate business. He also ran the Oregon Hotel in Redmond. Josephine died in 1927 and Frank in 1947. They are buried in the Redmond Cemetery.

DR. CASS A. CLINE was the first dentist in Central Oregon. In 1887, he left the Willamette Valley and came to the Deschutes River. The next year he opened a dental office in Prineville. He homesteaded above the Deschutes River at Cline Falls, which is named for him. He had to ride 23 miles to his dental office! The town of Cline Falls, which no longer exists, grew up around their homestead. Dr. Cline's wife was **EMILY M. CLINE**. She was born in 1868. The Cline's sold out and moved to Prineville. Later, they moved to Lower Bridge on the Deschutes River to farm and operate an inn for travelers. After another five years, the Clines moved to Redmond where Dr. Cline was a dentist. Dr. Cline died in 1926 and Emily in 1942. They are buried in the Redmond Cemetery.

GERTRUDE "TRUDY" MUNZ was not a pioneer of the Redmond region, but she had such an interesting history that she had to be included in this book. She was born a royal German princess named Helen Augusta Victoria Beatrice Bruckner Von Gotha on September 15, 1885 at Castle Liebenstein in Thuringen, Germany. The castle had 300 rooms. She traveled throughout Europe visiting the royal families, most of whom were related to her. Prince Albert of Great Britain was a relative, and she often visited Prince Albert and Queen Victoria, who was a cousin. The princess adopted the name Gertrude for herself. Her family was one of the wealthiest in Europe. Her father, Prince Oscar, was prime minister of the state.

In 1903 she met **ALFRED MUNZ,** a native of Switzerland who had established a hardware business in Minnesota. His sister was married to an officer of Prince Oscar's regiment. Alfred and Gertrude met at a royal ball and fell in love. Since Gertrude could not marry a commoner, she had to sign away all of her titles and property to marry Alfred. They had to leave Europe in 1904, to be married in New York. They lived in Minnesota for eight years before coming to Redmond in 1912 to run a hardware store. Her past life was kept a secret for many years. Alfred was born in 1865 and died March 2, 1940. Gertrude married Gus Bray in 1945. She died in 1966 and is buried in the Redmond Cemetery with her first husband.

ROBERT H. KRUG homesteaded at the south foot of Black Butte in the 1880's. He was murdered and burned in his cabin in the winter of 1917-1918. His grave is marked by his name dug into a small concrete block in the Camp Polk Cemetery. No dates are given.

JOHN BURR FRYREAR was born on December 19, 1832 (1833 on tombstone) in Kentucky. He came to Linn County in 1854. He married **ELIZABETH FRANCES BERRY** in 1858. She was born February 22, 1842 in Missouri. Her family moved to Linn County in 1853. In 1880 the Fryrear family took a farm northeast of Sisters on Squaw Creek. John was accidentally killed by a rolling log in a

hunting accident on September 27, 1919. Elizabeth died on November 27, 1926. The Fryrears are buried in the Camp Polk Cemetery near Sisters.

WILLIAM FRANCIS FRYREAR was a son of John and Elizabeth. He was born on May 9, 1866. He married **ETTA BELL TAYLOR** in 1886. She was born September 29, 1867 in California. She moved with her parents to the Sisters area sometime before 1886. The Fryrears had a farm six miles from Sisters on the old road to Redmond. They raised cattle and hay until the late 1920's, then they moved to a farm near Sunnyside, Washington. William died in September 1943 and Etta on April 12, 1952. They are buried in the Camp Polk Cemetery with both his and her parents.

JOHN TEMPLETON CRAIG spent many years promoting and building the first wagon road over McKenzie Pass. Before then, travelers had to use the terrible Scott Trail which was several miles to the south and a thousand feet higher in elevation. The only advantage of the Scott Trail was that it did not have to cross several miles of jagged lava flows. (These pioneer roads are described in the author's book *Pioneer Roads In Central Oregon.*) Craig's road went from McKenzie Bridge to Camp Polk near the present town of Sisters. The route was generally the same as present State Highway 242. Craig became president of his road company in 1871. The road over McKenzie Pass was open for traffic in 1872 as a toll road. After the road was open, a contract was let to carry mail from Eugene to Prineville. In 1877 Craig had the contract for the mail over the part of the route from McKenzie Bridge to Camp Polk. His first trip was in December 1877, but he never completed the journey. He was eventually found frozen to death in his cabin a few miles west of McKenzie Pass. He apparently was trying to start a fire but did not succeed. Craig was born in March 1821 and died just before Christmas 1877. He is buried beside the site of his cabin at the edge of State Highway 242.

Chapter 21

Klamath County Pioneers

WALLACE BALDWIN was the first white man to graze horses in Klamath County when he operated there in 1852. He was born October 6, 1833 in Philadelphia. He moved to St. Louis and then crossed the plains in 1850 to California. He ranged horses in the Klamath Falls area for about two years before settling at Talent in 1856. He was a second lieutenant under Captain Lindsay Applegate in the battle at Bloody Point near Tule Lake in 1861. He married Phoebe Alice Million in 1875. He moved to Linkville, which later became Klamath Falls, in 1884. He died on December 1, 1916 and is buried in the Klamath Falls Cemetery on the hill near the high school.

AMON SHOOK was born in Indiana on November 25, 1814. He moved to Iowa, and in 1864 crossed the plains to Jackson County. In 1869 he came to Klamath County south of Dairy. He married CATHERINE (KATHERINE on tombstone) YOST. She was born March 11, 1821 in Indiana. Amon died September 14, 1901 and Catherine on June 3, 1910. They are in the Klamath Falls Cemetery.

LUCIEN B. APPLEGATE was born April 24, 1842 in Missouri. He was the son of Lindsay Applegate. The Applegates came to Oregon in 1843, first to the Willamette Valley and then to the Ashland area where they operated a store. He helped his father locate the Klamath Agency and became superintendent of farming there for the Indians. In 1869 he moved to Swan Lake Valley eight miles northeast of Klamath Falls where he had 5000 acres of hay and grain and raised livestock. He became wealthy. He married MARGARET E. GRUBB in 1866. She was born in 1846 in Iowa and had crossed the plains in 1852 to the Rogue River Valley. During the Indian wars, Lucien was a major in the Oregon Volunteers. He died in 1926 and Margaret in 1925. They are buried in the pioneer Klamath Falls Cemetery near the high school.

CAPTAIN IVON (or IVAN) DECATUR APPLEGATE was born January 25, 1840 in Missouri. He was a son of Lindsay and Elizabeth Applegate. He arrived in Oregon in 1843. He moved to Yoncalla in 1850 and to Jackson County in 1860. In 1862, he settled at Ashland where he helped operate the Siskiyou Mountain Toll Road. He was in the party that rescued a wagon train from the Modoc Indians at Bloody Point in 1861. In 1863 he became captain of the State Militia at Ashland. He also raised stock with brother, Lucien. Ivon moved to Klamath County in 1869. He became an Indian agent to Chief Schonchin (or Sconchin) of the Modoc Indians. He was a leader in the Modoc War and fought in the battle at Lava Beds in January 1873. He married MARGARET HUTCHISON (HUTCHINSON on tombstone) in 1871. She was born in 1849. The Applegates raised stock. Ivon died December 28, 1918 and Margaret in 1926. They are buried in the Klamath Falls Cemetery.

CAPTAIN OLIVER CROMWELL APPLEGATE was born near Dallas on June 11, 1845. He too was a son of Lindsay Applegate. He moved to Douglas County and then to Ashland. He worked with his father at the Klamath Indian Agency. About 1870 he started raising cattle in Swan Lake Valley near Klamath Falls. He fought in the Modoc War of 1872-73 as captain of Company B, First Brigade, Oregon Volunteer Militia. Before that he was a captain of the State Militia at Ashland during the Civil War. He married Ella Anderson in Ashland in 1878. She was born October 30, 1855 near Talent. They moved to Klamath Falls in 1895. From 1898 to 1905 he was in charge of the Klamath Reservation. He died October 11, 1938 and lies in the pioneer Klamath Falls Cemetery.

JOSEPH CONGER was born May 11, 1822. He came to Linkville (later Klamath Falls) in 1868 as gardener for George Nurse. Nurse was the founder of Linkville and its first postmaster. Joe died February 2, 1908 and is buried in the Klamath Falls Cemetery.

CHARLES AUGUST LENZ was born in Germany on September 26, 1857. He came to Missouri and then to California to mine and operate a stage line. He came to Klamath County in 1884 and was the first settler north of the Klamath Agency. A railroad stop is named for him. In 1886 he married **ANNA** (**ANNIE B.** on tombstone) **CORBELL**. In addition to their ranch in northern Klamath County, they had a home in Klamath Falls. Charles died December 1, 1939 and Anna in 1969. They are buried in the Klamath Falls Cemetery.

There was a feud between the Calavan and the Laws families. H. G. Laws shot and killed Frank Calavan in 1882. Some time later on June 24, 1882, masked men assassinated **LEE LAWS** (aged 19) and **JOE LAWS** (aged 15), who were the children of H. G. and M. T. Laws. The boys are buried by a lilac bush at the south entrance to the pioneer Klamath Falls Cemetery.

FRANK TAZEWELL RIDDLE came from Kentucky in search of gold in northern California. He married **TOBY** (later called **WINEMA**) who was the daughter of a Modoc chief. In 1862 they were raising livestock north of Yreka, California. They moved to near Olene where he trapped for fur. Winema was a cousin of Captain Jack, the rebellious leader of the Modocs during the Modoc War. Both Frank and Winema were interpreters for the troops and peace commission during the war, and they were on many dangerous missions as they tried to bring peace between the whites and the Indians. After the war, they went on tour with the Indian agent, A. B. Meacham. Both Frank and Winema are buried in the Chief Sconchin Cemetery in the Sprague River Valley.

Chapter 22

Lake County Pioneers

Most of the early settlers of Lake County did not immigrate from the Willamette Valley, but instead they came from California by way of Susanville and Alturas. The little town of New Pine Creek on the California border was a busy place years before Lakeview came into existence. New Pine Creek is the oldest town in Lake County.

GEORGE W. CANNON was born in 1812. His wife was **MARY A. CANNON**, who was born in 1813. They took the Oregon Trail from Missouri to Polk County in 1853. George was the captain of the wagon train. They moved to the Umpqua Valley in 1854 and started a mill. They moved to Goose Lake Valley at New Pine Creek to be with their son in 1871. George died October 16, 1895, aged 83 years, 2 months, and 18 days. Mary died on March 24, 1894, aged 80 years, 6 months, and 18 days. They are buried in the New Pine Creek Cemetery.

CHRISTOPHER COLUMBUS CANNON was born in Missouri on February 11, 1842. He was the son of George and Mary Cannon. He came to Polk County with his parents in 1853. Christopher mined in Oregon, Idaho, and Washington from 1861 to 1869 when he came to the Goose Lake Valley. After seven years of operating a sawmill and raising stock, he moved to the town of New Pine Creek. He married **BLANCHE FOLLETTE** in 1887. She was the daughter of Captain E. and Christina Follette, who had come from Iowa to California and then to New Pine Creek. Christopher died in 1909 and Blanche in 1927. They are buried in the New Pine Creek Cemetery.

CAPTAIN ELIPHALET FOLLETTE (FOLLETT on tombstone) was born in 1828 and died in 1915. His wife was **CHRISTINA FOLLETTE**. She was born in 1833 and died in 1900. Their daughter, Blanche, married Christopher Columbus Cannon. Mr. and Mrs. Follette are buried in the New Pine Creek Cemetery. Also buried with them is **DYANTHA FOLLETTE (FOLLETT** on tombstone), who probably was Eliphalet Follette's mother. She was born October 8, 1806 and died October 15, 1897.

JOSEPH ROBNETTE (ROBNETT on tombstone) was one of the very early settlers near New Pine Creek where he started a flour mill in 1871. He was born in 1824 and died December 30, 1890, aged 66 years, 6 months, and 7 days. His wife was **MARY ROBNETTE**, who was born in 1828 and died October 2, 1889, aged 61 years, 11 months, and 1 day. They each have unusual tombstones in the New Pine Creek Cemetery.

JOHN O'NEIL was one of the first to settle in the Goose Lake Valley. He was born in 1842 and died in 1908. His wife was **NANCY O'NEIL**, who was born in 1852 and died in 1934. They are buried in the New Pine Creek Cemetery.

SOLOMON A. HAMMERSLEY was the first postmaster at New Pine Creek in 1872. He died January 10, 1898, aged 56 years, 25 days and is buried in the New Pine Creek Cemetery.

JAMES T. FITZGERALD was born June 3, 1830 in Tennessee. He married **SARAH E. NEIL** in 1851. She was born on June 14, 1832 in Tennessee. They moved to Missouri in 1859 from where he entered the army during the Civil War. They arrived in Jackson County, near Ashland in 1870. He fought in the Modoc War of 1872-73. They moved to Goose Lake in 1873 and settled five miles south of present Lakeview. He helped form Lake County from Jackson County in 1874. He also was a deputy sheriff for two years. James died August 26, 1906 and Sarah on March 30, 1908. They are in the New Pine Creek Cemetery.

JEZEREAL VENATOR was born March 12, 1814. He was raised in Tennessee and Illinois and crossed the plains in 1852 to Albany. He fought in the Rogue River War. He married **ELIZA MILLER,** who was born in Illinois. In 1870 they came to Goose Lake and started what may have been the first ranch in Lake County. Jezereal died of thirst while crossing the desert in Harney County in August 1880. Eliza died in 1914. They are buried in the Lakeview IOOF Cemetery.

WILLIAM HENRY DUKE was born in 1831. He married his second wife **ELIZABETH THURSTON** in 1869. After leaving Missouri, they settled seven and a half miles south of Lakeview in 1876. His son, **JAMES PATRICK DUKE** was born January 25, 1859 in Missouri. He married **MINNIE MYRTLE** in 1893. She was born south of New Pine Creek. The Duke families raised hay and cattle. Elizabeth was born November 14, 1838 and died July 18, 1899. Minnie was born in 1871 and died in 1961. William died in 1903 and James in 1933. All are buried in the Lakeview IOOF Cemetery.

ALBERT STEPHEN DOWN was born July 9, 1837 in Hastings, England. He became a sailor at ten years of age. He was in Sweden in 1855 and in Turkey in 1856. In 1858 he was a miner in Australia. He came to California in 1866 to log in the redwoods. He married **CARRIE ELIZABETH BALLARD** in 1870. She was born in 1853 and had crossed the plains to California in 1862. They moved to eleven miles west of Lakeview in 1879. In 1896 they moved to two and a half miles south of Lakeview. At first they raised sheep and later switched to cattle. Albert died in 1911 and Carrie in 1930. They are buried in the Lakeview IOOF Cemetery.

JAMES O. LATTA was the first person buried in the Lakeview IOOF Cemetery. He thought he was eating water cress, but it was poison hemlock. He died April 1, 1869, aged 48 years and 21 days at Deadman Creek.

HENRY R. HERYFORD was born July 29, 1850 in Missouri. He traveled to California by ox team in 1857. In 1872 he moved to the site of Lakeview with brothers, **WILLIAM P. HERYFORD** and James D. Heryford. They raised cattle just north of Lakeview. Henry married **MARY L. PARKER** in 1877. She was born January 25, 1859 in Iowa, but

moved to Jackson County in 1875. Henry died December 12, 1919 and Mary on January 9, 1957. William was born October 11, 1846 and died March 11, 1929. His wife was **MARY E. HERYFORD**. She was born November 3, 1854 and died May 31, 1931. The Heryfords are buried in the Lakeview IOOF Cemetery.

JAHIEL W. LOVELESS and brother, Charles, were the second families in the Lakeview area when they arrived in 1871. Jahiel was born in New York in 1829. His first wife was **EMMA A. LOVELESS** who died April 14, 1870, aged 22 years, 9 months, and 3 days. His second wife was **ROBERTIA A. LOVELESS,** a native of Missouri. She died December 4, 1889, aged 36 years, 1 month, and 4 days. Jahiel died May 1, 1901. The Loveless' are buried in the Lakeview IOOF Cemetery.

CHARLES U. SNIDER was born March 20, 1846 in Illinois. He and brother, A. Snider, opened the first store at the site of Lakeview. Charles died October 30, 1912 and is buried in the Lakeview IOOF Cemetery.

DR. BERNARD DALY was born February 17, 1858 in Ireland. He came to the United States and attended college in Ohio. He received a medical degree in Kentucky. He came to Lake County in 1887 to practice medicine. He was elected to the State Legislature in 1892 and to the State Senate in 1896. He became a county judge in 1902 and was the president of a Lakeview bank. He is most famous for his ride from Lakeview to Silver Lake after the disastrous Christmas eve fire of December 24, 1894 in which 43 people died. He undoubtedly saved the lives of many burn victims. Dr. Daly left his fortune to pay the college tuition of any graduate from Lake County high schools. He died in 1920 and has a magnificent monument in the Lakeview IOOF Cemetery.

CHARLES L. MITCHELL-INNES moved to the Paisley area from Scotland. He was of Scottish royalty and could have been an earl. He arrived at Paisley in 1874 and ran a store there until 1906. It is said that he gave Paisley its name. He died March 19, 1908 of Brights disease, aged 67 years. He is buried in the Paisley Cemetery.

JOHN BENTON BLAIR was born March 23, 1844 in Iowa. (His tombstone gives the date as April 21, 1843.) He arrived in Benton County in 1853. In 1872 he became one of the first settlers in the Chewaucan Valley. He was elected County assessor in 1900, and in 1901 he moved to Lakeview. He died May 31, 1929 and is buried in the Paisley Cemetery.

JOHN ALLEN WITHERS was born May 1, 1854 in Benton County. He was one of the first settlers in the Summer Lake area when he arrived in 1871 to raise cattle. He married Melvina Frances Hadley in 1875. Her family arrived in the same year that John had arrived. John settled nine miles northwest of Paisley where he had 1000 acres of hay and pasture land. He raised both cattle and sheep. He contracted smallpox and died March 27, 1902 and is buried in the Paisley Cemetery.

SAMUEL B. HADLEY was born on May 28, 1828. Another source states the date was May 10. He may have been the first settler at the site of Portland in the early 1840's. Other sources claim he crossed the plains in 1851 and settled in the Umpqua Valley. He and his family came to Summer Lake in 1871. His daughter Melvina married John Allen Withers. Samuel died on April 20, 1891 and is buried in the Paisley Cemetery.

WILLIAM ANDREW CURRIER was born in Corvallis October 12, 1851. In 1875 he came to 14 miles northwest of Paisley and settled in the Summer Lake area. He married **KITTY** (**KITTIE** on tombstone) **E. HADLEY** in 1875. She was another daughter of Samuel B. Hadley. She was born on July 7, 1862 in California. William became wealthy and owned 1700 acres, 2000 cattle, and over 1000 horses. He became a county commissioner and postmaster. William died in 1935 and Kitty in 1940. They are buried in the Paisley Cemetery.

JOHN BAGLEY was born December 8, 1826 in Arkansas. He married Lucretia Millsap in 1851. They crossed the plains to near Salem in 1854. They moved to Yreka, California in 1861 and then to Paisley in 1879. They ran a dairy and raised cattle and horses. John died December 15, 1890 and is buried in the Paisley Cemetery. Lucretia left Paisley and burned to death May 10, 1912.

JAMES HARVEY BONHAM was born December 4, 1838. He moved from Wisconsin to California and married **JANE** (called **JENNIE**) **ROBERTS** in 1871. She had walked all the way across the plains. She was born May 26, 1841. In 1875 the Bonhams moved to Summer Lake. In the 1890's they moved to the east side of the Lake. James died June 8, 1911 and Jennie on May 23, 1925. They are buried in the Summer Lake Cemetery a few miles south of the village of Summer Lake.

JAMES FOSTER was born July 4, 1827. In 1845 he crossed the plains with the Tetherow group of Meek's Lost Wagon Train to Forest Grove. Later he moved to near Corvallis. He married **ELIZABETH B. CURRIER,** who was born on June 18, 1832 in Vermont. She lived in Massachusetts, New York, and Missouri before coming to Oregon in 1846 by the Applegate Trail. They were married in 1848. In 1871, James took 125 head of cattle to the Summer Lake area and built a cabin at Paisley. The whole family moved to Summer Lake in 1873. They had 15 children. Frederick Butte is named for one of their sons. In 1888, they moved from Foster Creek to the mouth of Ana River and raised livestock and race horses. James died December 19, 1909 of pneumonia, and Elizabeth died June 12, 1921. They are buried in the Summer Lake Cemetery. One of their sons, **RALPH CURRIER FOSTER** was born November 7, 1874 at Summer Lake. It was reported that he was an outlaw part of his life and was involved with the masked gang that killed about 3000 sheep at Christmas Lake on February 3, 1904. He also was with the group that killed about 2500 sheep 25 miles east of Christmas Lake on April 29, 1904. He might have been involved in the murder of store owner, J. C. Conn, of Silver Lake who knew who had bought the ammunition for the killing of the sheep. Ralph died December 1, 1961 and is buried in the Summer Lake Cemetery.

JAMES MONROE SMALL was born July 27, 1850 in Missouri. He crossed the plains to Lane County. James was one of the first settlers to Chewaucan Valley in 1873. He had married **CELESTE MAUD BRATTAIN,** who was born in 1860. They moved to Silver Lake in 1886 where their son,

Robert, died in the 1894 Christmas eve fire. The Smalls moved to Summer Lake in 1908. James died in 1932 and Maud on July 3, 1937. They have a giant monument in the Paisley Cemetery.

MICHEAL SULT was born July 1, 1847 in Ohio. He lived in Indiana and Missouri before coming to Lane County in 1869. He settled in the Summer Lake Valley in 1872 at the site of the Summer Lake Cemetery. He married **LAURA BELL CONRAD** in 1861. They raised fruit, grain, alfalfa, and cattle. Mike died August 11, 1917 and Bell on February 6, 1941. They are buried in the Summer Lake Cemetery.

THOMAS JEFFERSON BRATTAIN was born in Illinois on January 2, 1829. He married **PERMELIA JANE GILLESPIE,** who was born in Missouri on June 4, 1838. They crossed the plains to Lane County in 1852. Tom was a sheriff of Lane County, and later he was the first sheriff of Lake County. In 1869 they moved to the Langell Valley near Klamath Falls, and in 1870 they moved to Bonanza. They settled in the Chewaucan Valley in 1873. In 1876 he was postmaster of the first post office in the Paisley area. He started a hotel and a livery stable at Paisley in 1878. Tom died December 3, 1909 and Permelia on June 11, 1913. They are in the Paisley Cemetery.

GEORGE C. DUNCAN was born October 23, 1827. His wife was **LOUISA DUNCAN,** who was born on September 10, 1832. They were early settlers in the Silver Lake area. He established the first post office in the area east of the present town of Silver Lake in 1874. He died March 10, 1909 and she on January 3, 1884. They are in the Silver Lake Cemetery.

ALONZO WELCH LONG was born in 1848, and his wife, **MARY JANE LONG** was born in 1862. They lived at Jacksonville and raised cattle. They also raised cattle in Lake County. Alonzo was a volunteer in the Bannock War. The Indians killed all of his cattle. They moved to Lakeview where he worked on ranches in the area. He also freighted from Lakeview to California and operated a livery stable in Lakeview. In 1900 they moved to Christmas Valley to homestead. Alonzo died in 1919 and Mary in 1949. They are buried in the Silver Lake Cemetery. Their son, **REUBEN A. LONG,** was a rancher in the Fort Rock area and was known as the Sage of the Desert because of his stories and dry humor. Reub was born in 1898 and died in 1974. He is buried in the Fort Rock Cemetery.

Part 2

Pioneer Barns

The hand-hewn beams of the Hindman barn were held together by wood pegs.

The owner of the barn dismantled it with the hope of restoring it. Politics and vandalism prevented the restoration. This photo shows some of the hand-hewn beams that held up the barn.

An old barn at Hardman that will not last much longer.

The pioneer barn at Peter French's famous P Ranch near Frenchglen.
French was one of the great "cattle kings" of the West.

Stage barn on the Rufner Ranch on the pioneer road between Shaniko and Prineville.

The round barn on the famous Hay Creek Ranch east of Madras. Hay Creek Ranch was on the pioneer road between Shaniko and Prineville.

Samuel M.W. Hindman came to Camp Polk near Sisters in 1869 or '70. He built a barn in 1871 which was the oldest pioneer building in Deschutes County until it was destroyed.

A storm during the winter of 1989-'90 partly destroyed the Hindman barn.

This barn was at a stage stop on the Steens Wagon Road on Combs Flat southeast of Prineville.
This barn collapsed during the 1980's and no longer exists.

The Prindle barn south of Fossil. The Prindles were early pioneers at Fossil.
The original part of the barn was constructed with square nails.

The barn at the Beech Creek Stage Station south of the town of Fox. The barn was on the pioneer road between Long Creek and John Day.

An old barn at the Hog Flat Stage Station on the road between Fox and John Day.

The old barn at the Cold Camp Stage Station southeast of Antelope. This barn was on the pioneer road between The Dalles and Canyon City during the gold rush days of the 1860's.

The Mt. Vernon horse fort. This building was built in 1871 to protect the famous stallion, Mt. Vernon. The building was on the pioneer road from The Dalles to Canyon City. It is located east of the town of Mount Vernon.

The Hill Beachy stage barn at the Ruby Ranch west of Jordan Valley during the 1980's.
This barn was on the pioneer road between Silver City, Idaho and Winnemucca.

By 1991, the Hill Beachy stage barn had collapsed.

Abandoned Schools

Before the days of the automobile, school children had to walk or ride a horse to get to school. This limited the distance from home to school to about five miles or less. Thus, the rural areas were covered with hundreds of schools which have been abandoned. Many of these schools still stand in areas where no one lives today as the early settlers left and the land was taken over by large ranches or farms.

The Eightmile Schoolhouse was on the Barlow Road and the pioneer road between
The Dalles and Dufur (top and bottom photographs).

The Lost Prairie School is north of Flora.

The McKay Creek School is northeast of Prineville.

Oregon Canyon School near Oregon Canyon Ranch northwest of McDermitt.

Smith Mountain School on top of Smith Mountain north of Wallowa.

The Flanagan School was on the pioneer Bakeoven Road. It is near the present highway between Maupin and Shaniko.

The Klondike School is southeast of Wasco.

The Combs Flat School is on the Steens Wagon Road southeast of Prineville. It may be the oldest school still standing in Crook County.

The Waldron School is near Richmond on the highway between Mitchell and Service Creek.

The Clarno School is at Clarno, just west of the Deschutes River.

Lower Pine Creek School on the highway east of Clarno.

Clem School near railroad stop at Clem between Condon and Arlington.

Top School northeast of Monument.

School at south end of Fox Valley.

Virginia Valley School near State 78 between Burns and Burns Junction.

Pine Valley School at Halfway.

Homestead School along Snake River north of Oxbow Dam.

Flora School.

Paradise School.

The Howard School is east of Prineville on Ochoco Creek.

The Friend School is near the hamlet of Friend.

Deer Creek School at Paradise. This school was remodeled and only recently abandoned.

Freezeout School on Imnaha River south of Imnaha.

Homesteads

At the turn of the twentieth century, many home-steaders moved into the High Desert and other regions of eastern Oregon. Most of the homes were of simple construction. Many of the homes had one or two rooms on the first floor and sleeping quarters on the second floor, which was reached by ladder or stairs.

There was a homestead at Dickerson Well south of Brothers. It was abandoned long ago, and the house will soon disappear.

Even stone buildings eventually collapse. This one is north of Bogan on the pioneer Dalles Military Road.

Larry Palmer by homesteaders home in Sweetmilk Canyon.

An abandoned homestead on the Bakeoven Road between Maupin and Shaniko.

A homestead north of Shaniko.

Water was a major problem on the High Desert, and it led to the downfall of most of the homesteaders. A frame for a windmill still stands at Dickerson Well, which was on the pioneer road between Prineville and Lakeview.

Abandoned
Churches

The church at Lonerock stands beside the rock that gave the town its name.

A homestead south of Fox is ready to collapse.

Old homes and buildings at Beech Creek south of Fox.

The Claus Johnson home on Hale Ridge in the Hardman area.

Some homes of the homestead area were substantial structures such as this one a mile west of Westfall.
But, they too fade away unless taken care of.

The church at Locust Grove west of Wasco. Buildings disintegrate
rapidly once holes develop in the roof and the doors and windows let
the rain into the building.

Richmond church is still used once a year.

A beautiful old church in Grass Valley.

An old church in Drewsey.

The church in Wapinitia is used to store hay and is rapidly falling apart.

The church at Flora.

Old Pumps

Just about every homestead had to have a pump to supply water for the household. These pumps were nearly always outside the house, not inside.

This pump is at the Bowden Ranch north of McDermitt along the pioneer road between Fort McDermitt and Silver City, Idaho.

This pump supplied water to a homestead west of Westfall.

The ghost town of Ashwood is the location of this pump. This pump is designed for shallow wells of about 28 feet or less.

With the coming of the automobile, every town had to have a service station and a gas pump. Some of these gas pumps still exist. A hand lever pumps the gas from a storage tank to the glass tank on top. Marks along the glass tank indicate how much gas was bought.

Long Creek had this pump.

The ghost town of Starkey also has a pump.

The ghost town of Beulah once had a gas pump.

Pioneer Roads

Lawrence Nielsen on pioneer road south of Olex.

Deanne Nielsen on a stone wall on the
Sherars Road.

Ruts on the road between Pilot Rock and Hepner.

Looking down Sweetmilk Canyon.

Grooves worn in rock by wagons on Willamette Valley and Cascade Mountain Military Road west of Lower Bridge and Deschutes River.

Miscellaneous

Haying was a very labor-intensive operation until fairly recent times. First, the hay was cut with a mowing machine. A rake put the hay in windrows. A man with a pitch fork put the hay into piles called shocks. One or two men pitched the shocks into a wagon which carried the hay to a stack. There were many kinds of homemade stackers used to move the hay from the wagon to the hay stack with a Jackson fork. The Jackson fork had three foot tines and had a steel cable attached to the stacker. The other end of the steel cable was attached to a derrick horse that lifted the Jackson fork with a load of hay from the wagon. The load of hay swung around over the stack and at the right moment, the man in the wagon jerked a rope which dumped the hay on the stack.

Boyd was once a thriving community south of The Dalles. Most of its buildings have disappeared or are rotting away.

The Nansenes Dance Hall was on the pioneer road between The Dalles and Sherars Bridge.
Today this hall is on the Tye Ridge Road.

Waldron was a small hamlet between Richmond and Mitchell. The old community hall leaned badly for years.

Finally the Waldron Community hall collapsed in 1990.

Around the turn of the century many of the homesteaders moved to the area north of the town of Brothers. These settlers built a dance hall about 11 miles north of Brothers to celebrate Christmas and other holidays. Katie Rockwell was one of these homesteaders. Previously she had gained fame and notoriety as the leading dance hall girl in the Klondike and was known as "Queen of the Yukon." Her name was inscribed on the west wall of the building December 25, 1914. The Pringle Hall dance hall is rapidly deteriorating.

Logs were carried from the forest to the saw mills in Bend by railroads instead of by trucks. Once the logs were removed the tracks were abandoned. These two photos show the rotting ties of a Shevlin logging contract. New trees quickly sprang up between old ties.

Twickenham was a small hamlet along the John Day River. Not much remains except a picturesque Hotel.

The town of Dayville once had a beautiful Hotel—built sometime around 1890. It burned in June 1984.

In the early 1900's railroads were built on both sides of the Deschutes River toward Bend. Later the railroad on the east side of the river was abandoned. A large tressel was built across Gordon Creek a few miles south of the Columbia River. Gordon Canyon is in the background and the Deschutes River is in the foreground. In the 1980's this tressel was destroyed by a range fire. The Dalles Military Road split at this point, one branch going up Gordon Creek and the other branch going to the right.

The Columbia Southern railroad went from Biggs to Shaniko. This road reached Shaniko in 1900 and once hauled an immense quantity of wool and grain to market. Today the tracks are abandoned but traces of the old railroad bed can be seen in places. The photo shows the rotting ties of the abandoned track a few miles north of Shaniko.

In this photo, Deanne Nielsen examines one type of hay stacker and a Jackson fork west of Drewsey.

Fordson tractors were popular in the 1920's. They could pull loads, or they could be used to drive other machinery such as stationary threshers with a take-off for a belt. This abandoned tractor is west of Drewsey.

Old Chief Joseph's boundary marker on Minum Hill. This monument was built in 1863. It did not keep the white man out of the Wallowa Valley.

Stock driveways are seldom used now. Livestock are now transported by truck. Parts of the Prineville-Mitchell Road later became a stock driveway. The stock driveways were marked by signs nailed to ponderosa pine trees.

Drag log from Meeks Lost wagon train near Camp Creek. This Juniper log was cut in 1845 and tied behind a wagon to act as a brake on a steep slope. This dragline is in a preserve at the Bowman Museum in Prineville.

In the background are the ruts of General Howards troops who came down to Jackass Creek from a spar of Jackass Mountain just below Dry Branch of the south fork of the John Day River. The ruts are caused by rough-locking of the wheels of the wagons and the cannon during the Bannock War of 1878.

In 1884 Mark Anthony Carson and his wife Elizabeth Strickland Carson settled near the junction of Camp Creek and Crooked River. Their log cabin with a large stone fireplace became the Maury Stage Station where horses were changed on the stages and travelers could get food and lodging. The station still stands between Post and Paulina. It was also a post office.

The abandoned railroad tressel at Gordon Canyon was destroyed by a range fire in the 1980's.

The McGirr Store in Fox. Typical of the times it was built with a false front. McGirr homesteaded in 1879.

Old building in Danner.

The Hay Creek Ranch near Madras was one of the world's largest sheep ranches.
It had a large commissary to supply the needs of the ranch hands and nearby settlers.

Ruins of Inskip (Inskeep) Stage Station west of Jordan Valley.
The square hole in the stone wall is a rifle port in this fortified station.

Sign in Inskip Station (Innskip)

Outdoor toilets at Wapinitia.

This is an iron hitching loop at the A.J. Tetherow House at Tetherow Crossing.
The loop was driven into a Lombardy poplar tree. Later vandals stole the loop.

IN SEARCH OF OUR FADING PAST

What brought them West, those pioneers of old?
Was it adventure, freedom, or a vision of gold?
Some found gold in a cultivated crop,
More sought gold from pounding the rock.
Farmers were happy to till soil in the hollow,
Wherever man moved, services would follow.
The blacksmith, the merchant, the soldiers who fought,
They crafted their needs when none could be bought.
Most asked for little, most received same,
Their simple tombstones give date and name.
Many are forgotten, a few achieved fame,
Is all history lost from whence they came?
Don't you believe it, for new pioneers
Are searching for facts forgotten for years.
And if you look carefully, you too can see
Clues from the past as things used to be.
Starting with a "ghost town" is an easy beginning,
For the sturdiest buildings may still be standing.
The most basic needs for those near and far
Were the mercantile, the hotel, the livery and bar.
The church drew followers from endless miles,
Their faith born of many hardships and trials.
Sun reflects on a cemetery by the side of a hill,
Dates prove many too young for their dreams to fulfill.
Schoolhouses were built, but not always in town,
Many stood isolated with no buildings around.
A lonesome old barn stands surrounded by weeds,
Reminding us that life could depend on good steeds.
Women left subtle clues to catch the eye,
In the sagebrush, bachelor buttons wave to the sky.
An old lilac bush blooms close to a stream
Where rubble of a stage stop still can be seen.
All things were connected by one common thread.
The ruts of the wagons in the old roadbed.
So, as you go driving down roads, try to see
The crumbling, fading past of our history.

References and Further Reading

Mildretta Adams, *Sagebrush Post Offices*, Idaho State Univ. Press, Pocatello, 1986.

An Illustrated History of Union and Wallowa Counties, Western Historical Publishing Co., 1902.

Barbara Ruth Bailey, *Main Street Northeastern Oregon*, Ore. Historical Soc., 1982.

Baker County Hist. Soc., *The History of Baker County*, 1986.

Irene Barklow, *The Old and The New—History of Post Offices in Wallowa County*, Maverick, 1982.

Irene Barklow, *From Trails To Rails: Post Offices, Stage Stops, and Wagon Roads of Union County, Oregon*, Maverick, 1987.

Grace Bartlett, "Origin of Wallowa County Names," Unpublished manuscript, Wallowa Co. Library, Enterprise.

Grace Bartlett, *The Wallowa Country: 1867-1877*, Self published, 1976.

F. Lorlene Beddow, *"Carving The North End Wilderness: Flora,"* Privately published, Pendleton, 1985.

Peter G. Boag, Ashwood On Trout Creek, Ore. Hist. Quarterly, *91*, 117, 1990.

George F. Brimlow, *The Bannock Indian War of 1878*, Caxton Printers, Caldwell, Idaho, 1938.

George F. Brimlow, *Harney County Oregon and Its Range Land*, Binford and Mort, 1951.

George F. Brimlow, Two Cavalrymen's Diaries of the Bannock War, 1878, Ore. Hist. Quarterly, *68*, 221, 293, 317 (1967).

Phil Brogan, "Carroll Cemetery" Ore. Hist. Quarterly, *73*, 228 (1972).

Phil Brogan, *East of the Cascades*, Binford and Mort, Portland, 1964.

D. Ordell Calkins, *Ione and Us*, Artprint Press, Sacramento, California, 1982.

Arthur H. Campbell, "Charlie Clarno and The John Day Queen," Ore. Hist. Quarterly, *88*, 349 (1987)

Arthur H. Campbell, *The Clarno Era*, Unpublished manuscript, 1976.

Arthur H. Campbell, *John Day River—Drift and Historical Guide*, Frank Amato Publ., Portland, 1980.

Arthur H. Campbell, *Antelope: The Saga Of A Western Town*, Maverick, Bend, 1989.

Keith Clark, *Redmond: Where The Desert Blooms*, Ore. Hist. Soc. Portland, 1985.

Vira Cordano, *Levi Scott—Oregon Trailblazer*, Binford and Mort, 1982.

Crook Co. Hist. Soc., *Echoes From Old Crook County*, Prineville, 1991.

Deschutes Co. Hist. Soc., *A History of the Deschutes County in Oregon*, Redmond, 1985.

E.A. Donnell, Rowe Creek, 1890-91: Mary L. Fitzmaurice Diary, Ore. Hist. Quarterly, *83*, 171, 288, 1982.

James R. Evans, *Gold Dust and Chalk Dust*, Baker Printing, 1981.

John W. Evans, *Powerful Rockey*, Eastern Oregon St. Coll., La Grande, 1991.

Theressa Foster, *Settlers In Summer Lake Valley*, Maverick, 1989.

Giles French, *The Golden Land*, Ore. Hist. Soc., 1958.

Giles French, *Homesteads and Heritages: A History of Morrow County, Oregon*, Binford and Mort, 1971.

Friends of the La Pine Library, *History of the La Pine Pioneers*, Sagebrush Printing, Bend, 1983.

Ralph Friedman, *In Search of Western Oregon*, Caxton Printers, 1990.

Gregory M. Franzua, *The Oregon Trail Revisited*, Patrice Press, St. Louis, Mo.

Friends of the Maupin Library, *Chaff In the Wind*, 1986.

F. Smith Fussner, *Glimpses of Wheeler County's Past*, Binford and Mort, 1975.

Genealogical Forum of Portland, Oregon, Yesterday's Roll Call. List of burials in Umatilla, Baker, and Sherman Counties, 1970.

H. Dean Guie, *Bugles In the Valley: Garnett's Fort Simcoe*, Republic Press, Yakima, 1956.

Gilliam County Hist. Soc., *History of Gilliam County, Oregon*, Condon, 1981.

Edward Gray, *An Illustrated History Of Early Northern Klamath County, Oregon*, Maverick, 1989.

Jacob Ray Gregg, *Pioneer Days In Malheur County*, Los Angeles, 1950.

Bruce Harris, *The History of Wasco County*, Oregon Hist. Soc., 1983.

I. Hiatt, *Thirty-One Years In Baker County*, Abbott and Foster, Baker, 1893.

Hood River Co. Hist. Soc., *History of Hood River County* Vol. I and II., 1982 and 1987.

Bernal D. Hug, *History of Union County, Oregon*, Eastern Ore. Rev., Union Co. Hist. Soc., La Grande, 1961.

Royal Jackson and Jennifer Lee, *Harney County—An Historical Inventory*, Harney Co. Hist. Soc., 1978.

Jefferson Co. Hist. Soc., *History of Jefferson County*, Madras.

Lee C. Johnson, *A Brief History of Union County*.

Frances Juris, *Old Crook County—The Heart of Oregon*, Prineville Print Shop, 1975.

Will M. Kidwell, *In The Footsteps Of The Pioneers*, San Diego, Ca., 1983.

John F. Kilkenney, *Shamrocks and Shepherds: The Irish of Morrow County*, Ore. Hist. Soc., 1969

Fred Lockley, *Conversations With Bullwhackers & Muleskinners*, Rainy Day Press, Eugene, 1981.

Fred Lockley, *Conversations With Pioneer Women*, Rainy Day Press, Eugene, 1981.

L.A. McArthur, *Oregon Geographic Names*, Ore. Hist. Soc., Portland, Ore.

Sam McMillan, *The Bunchgrassers*, Irwin-Hudson Co., 1974.

William H. McNeal, *History of Wasco County*, Self published, 1933.

Many Hands, *Jefferson County Reminiscences*, Binford and Mort, 1957.

Morrow Co. Hist. Soc., *History of Morrow County, Oregon*, 1983.

Lawrence Nielsen, *In The Ruts Of The Wagon Wheels*, Maverick, Bend, 1987.

Lawrence Nielsen, D. Newman and G. McCort, *Pioneer Roads In Central Oregon*, Maverick, Bend, 1985.

Lawrence Nielsen, *Roads Of Yesterday In Northeastern Oregon*, Maverick, 1990.

H. Oliver, *Gold and Cattle Country*, Binford and Mort, 1961.

Oregon Dept. of Transportation, Oregon Cemetery Survey, Salem, 1978.

Oregon Soc. D.A.R., "Oregon Historic Landmarks, Eastern Oregon," 1959.

Ft. Rock Valley Hist. Soc., *Portraits: Ft. Rock Valley Homestead Years*, Helen Parks, Ed., Maverick Publ., 1989.

Col. Wm. Parsons and W.S. Shiach, *An Illustrated History of Umatilla County and of Morrow County*, W.H. Lever, Publisher, 1902.

Pat Phillips, "The Family of Eleazar Gilliam and Nancy Jane Robbins Gilliam," Privately printed, 1990.

Pioneer Ladies Club, *Reminiscences of Oregon Pioneers*, East Oregonian Publ. Co., Pendleton, 1937.

Miles F. Potter, *Oregon's Golden Years*, Caxton Printers, Caldwell, Id., 1978.

Helen Guyton Rees, *Shaniko*, Binford and Mort, Portland, 1982.

Mildred Searcey, *Way Back When*, East Oregonian Publishing Co., Pendleton, 1972.

Jeanne M. Secord, *Yesterday In Grant County*, Blue Mtn. Eagle, John Day, 1973.

Elinor Cohn Shank, "Looking Back at Hepner," Ore. Hist. Quarterly, *91*, 378, (1990).

F.A. Shaver, et at., *An Illustrated History of Central Oregon*, Western Historical Publishing Co., Spokane, Wa., 1905.

Roscoe Sheller, *Ben Snipes: Northwest Cattle King*, Binford and Mort, Portland, 1957.

L. Sisemore, Ed., *History of Klamath, Oregon*, Klamath Falls, 1941.

Gordon and Patricia Stewart, *Baker County Sketch Book*, The Record-Courier, Baker

Janet and McLaren Stinchfield, Ed., *The History of Wheeler County, Oregon*, The Times-Journal, Condon, 1983.

Alma Jean Tipley, Sherman Co: For The Record, Sherman Co. Hist. Soc., 7, #2, 1989.

Charles H. Voegtly, *An Illustrated History of Baker, Grant, Malheur and Harney Counties*, Western Hist. Publ. Co., 1902.

Wallowa Co. Museum, *History of Wallowa County, Oregon*, Enterprise, 1983.

B. Elizabeth Ward, *Redmond, Rose Of The Desert*, Midstate Printing, Redmond, 1975.

Marion T. Weatherford, *Arlington*, Ore. Hist. Soc., 1977.

Index

Keeney, Thomas B. 30
Kees Cemetery 2, 6, 64
Keith, Lydia O. 14 - 15
Kernan, William 89
Kerns, Mary L. 18
Ketchum, Alwilda "Wilda" 99
Keyes, Rebecca Jane 27
Kilcup, Ada 59
Kilcup, Edward W. 59
Kilgore, Louisa A. Poole 18
Kirk, Alex 64
Kirk, Anne 64
Kirk, Frances 68
Kirk, Thomas J. 64
Klamath Falls Cemetery 6, 123 - 124
Klinger, Caroline 24
Klinger, Louis J. 16
Knighten, Ida J. 59
Knotts, Carrie 61
Knotts, Isaac 61 - 62
Knotts, Perry O. 61
Knotts, Rachel 61
Knotts, William 61
Koontz, Echo 64
Koontz, James H. 64
Krug, Robert H. 122
Kuhl, Peter 30

L

LaFollette, Jerome B. 98
Lakeview IOOF Cemetery 126
Langdon, Lucius 101
Latta, James O. 126
Laughlin, Elizabeth 9
Laughlin, Mary 9
Laughlin, William C. 9
Lavadour, Joseph 6
Lavadour, Lisette 6
Laws, H. G. 124
Laws, Joe 124
Laws, Lee 124
Laws, M. T. 124
Leach, Rebecca 119
Ledford, Elizabeth 18
Ledford, John M. 18
Lehman, James 63

Lenz, Charles August 124
Leonard, Daniel G. 21, 24
Leonard, Frances 21, 24
Lewis and Clark Expedition 3
Lexington Cemetery 59
Lexington Penland Cemetery 58
Lieuallen, Sarah E. 64
Lieuallen, Thomas Tyndall 64
Lincoln, Abraham 62
Lindsay, Nathaniel 21
Littlefield, David S. 69
Littlepage, Agnes P. 62
Lockett, Robert A. 92
Logan, Thomas Jefferson 100
Logan, William L. 91
Lone Pine (Wamic) Cemetery 16
Long Creek Cemetery 30, 55
Long, Alonzo Welch 128
Long, Mary Jane 128
Long, Reuben A. 128
Lord, Wentworth 9
Lost Prairie Cemetery 89
Lovejoy, A. J. 25
Loveless, Charles 126
Loveless, Emma A. 126
Loveless, Jahiel W. 126
Loveless, Robertia A. 126
Lovgren, Albert Peter 59
Lovgren, Johanna Sophia 59
Lucas, George Washington 18
Luce, Jane 29
Luckman, Emma 59
Lyle, James O. 10
Lyle, Washington Cemetery 1, 12
Lytle, Andrew 98

M

Madden Jr., John 22
Madden, Alma 22
Madden, George 22
Madden, John 22
Madras Cemetery 102, 120
Maling, Charles Cooper 120
Mansfield, Elizabeth 6
Marlatt, Thomas 59
Marlatt, Wesley 59

Marsh, Louisa (Meeker) 25
Marsh, Mary E. 25
Marsh, Walter 25
Martin, Mary Jane 94
Martin, Sarah M. 89 - 90
Mascal, Richard 56
Mascal, Sophia J. 56
Masiker, George 20
Masiker, Palmyra Elizabeth Trumble 20
Mason, John 15
Mason, Sylvester W. 14 - 15
Masonic Cemetery 11
Masouart, Mary 15
Masouart, Nicholas 15
Masterson, Lucy Jane 97
Maupin Cemetery 19, 102, 119
Maupin, Howard 18 - 19, 119
Maupin, Nancy A. 97 - 98
May, Elizabeth Matilda 101
Mayes, James D. 102
Mayes, Sarah E. 102
Mayo, Carl 95
Mays, Lodema 15
Mays, Robert 15
Mayville Cemetery 25
McAtee, Benjamin C. 17
McAtee, Phoebe A. 17
McAtee, Sarah 17
McAtee, W. H. 17
McBroom, Albert 62
McBroom, Celia E. 63
McBroom, Ella 62
McClure, Nancy Ellen (Ella) 57
McCoin, Julius S. 99
McConnell, Martha 16
McConnell, Phoebe (Phebe) 25
McCorkle, William Milton 16
McCormack, Lutheria 90
McCormack, William M. 90
McCoy, Olney 63
McCrary, Elizabeth E. 70
McCrary, William F. 70
McCullum, Nancy 18 - 19
McFarland, William Robert 97
McGirr, Frank 55
McGowan, George 94
McKay, Dr. William 65
McLaughlin, Dr. John 65

Shook, Amon 123
Siandeker, Jemima 6
Silver Creek Cemetery 95
Silver Lake Cemetery 128
Sinnott, Col. N. B. 12
Sinnott, Nicholas J. 12
Sipe, Elizabeth 89
Slusher, Thomas W. 14
Smailes, Elizabeth 19
Small, James Monroe 127 - 128
Small, Robert 128
Smith, Alex 23 - 24
Smith, Anderson C. 87 - 88
Smith, Joseph 24
Smith, Mary Ann 27
Smith, Mrs. Eliza J. 57
Smith, Nancy M. 26
Smith, Perlina 70
Smith, Sarah 92
Smith, T. B. 8
Smith, Three Fingered 66
Smith, William 96
Snider, A. 126
Snider, Charles U. 126
Snider, Harriet 12
Snipes Jr., Ben 10
Snipes, Asenath 10
Snipes, Ben 10
Snipes, Elam 10
Snipes, George R. 10
Snipes, Martha 10
Snodderly, Nancy Ellen 30
Snoderly, James H. 99
Sommerville, Alexander 68
South Kingsley Cemetery 17
Southern, Charles H. 15
Southern, Elizabeth A. 15
Southern, Martin 15
Spalding, H. H. 98
Spalding, Martha J. 98
Sperry, J. L. 8
St. Andrews Mission Cemetery 6
St. Joseph Cemetery 23, 25
St. Peters Cemetery 9, 11 - 12
Staats, William H. 14, 121
Staley, Hezekiah 18
Stanclift, George M. 99 - 100
Stanclift, Mary C. (Hill) 99 - 100
Stanfield, Robert Nelson 64

Stanley, James J. 89
Stark, Margaret 92
Stark, William K. (or S.) 92
Steele, General 55
Steers, James Francis Marion 17
Stenger, Peter F. 94
Stewart, Anne C. 61
Stewart, Eli 61
Stewart, Harold 61
Stinchfield, Edmund Alphonso 25
Stone, Nancy 6
Straud, Mary A. 26
Strock, Mary E. 89
Stuart, Elizabeth 21
Stubblefield, R. F. 88
Sturgill, Mary A. 68
Sturtevant, Andrew Jackson 61
Sult, Michael 128
Summer Lake Cemetery 127 - 128
Summers, Mary Ellen 25
Summerville Cemetery 68

T

Tarter, A. M. 67
Tarter, Nicholas 67
Taylor, Etta Bell 122
Teel, Dr. John 63
Teel, Nancy Jane 63
Templeton, David 97
The Dalles IOOF Cemetery 9 - 14, 16, 18 - 19, 26, 28
The Dalles Pioneer Cemetery 13, 21
Thompson, James 92
Thompson, Lydia Ann 92
Thompson, William "Billy" G. 92
Thomson, Camilla 11
Thurston, Elizabeth 126
Toby 124
Todd, John Y. 15
Tomlinson, Dulcina 96
Toney, Effie Blanch 97
Tower, Harriet N. 88
Tower, Martha E. 87

Townsend, Hattie 64
Trimble, David B. 23
Trimble, Eliza Z. 23
Trowbridge, Bradford C. 29
Tucker, Emma Louise 64
Turnage, Mary 17
Turpin, Emma A. 121
Tygh Valley Cemetery 16 - 17

U

Umatilla Cemetery 64
Underhill, Amos 21
Union Cemetery 8, 66 - 68
Unsel, Margaret 17

V

Vale Pioneer Cemetery 91 - 92
Vale's Valley View Cemetery 93
Vanadevert, Walter 97
Vanderpool, Dr. Larkin 17
Vandevert, Charles 97
Vandevert, Grace 121
Vandevert, Jackson J. 97, 121
Vandevert, William Plutarch 121
Vandevort, Joshua Jackson 121
Vanina Fulgenzio 98
Venator, Alphena 94 - 95
Venator, Elizabeth 94
Venator, Ira K. 95
Venator, Jezreel (or Jezereal) 94, 125 - 126
Venator, Josephine 95
Venator, Luella 95
Vey, John 8
Vey, Joseph 8
Vey, Tony 8
Vincentheller, Sadie Lee 121
Von Gotha, Princess Helen 122

W

Wade, Martha Ann (Stephenson Garlett) 24
Wade, William Nash 24

LAWRENCE E. NIELSEN

Lawrence E. Nielsen was raised on a cattle, sheep, and wheat ranch south of Pilot Rock along the pioneer road between Pilot Rock and Granite. His father and his mother's father had both homesteaded in the area.

He graduated from Pacific University, Washington State University, and Cornell University from which he received a Ph.D. Degree in chemistry and physics. He spent over 32 years doing research on plastics and composite materials for the Monsanto Company. This research resulted in about 150 publications, six patents, and five technical books. He received two national awards and a listing in *Who's Who In America*. Dr. Nielsen was an Affiliate Professor in chemical engineering at Washington University in St. Louis for seven years.

Larry has been on 19 mountain climbing and glacier research expeditions to Alaska and the Yukon Territory. In 1959, Larry led the first expedition to retrace the gold rush route of 1898 over the Valdez Glacier in Alaska. Many artifacts were found melting out of the glacier ice.

When he retired in the spring of 1977, Larry began retracing pioneer roads in Oregon east of the Cascade Mountains. This has been nearly a full time job for over 13 years. This road research has resulted in the publication of the books *Pioneer Roads In Central Oregon* and *In The Ruts Of The Wagon Wheels: Pioneer Roads In Eastern Oregon. Roads Of Yesterday* is the third book in this series.

Larry is married to Deanne M. Boss. Their daughter, Linda, is married to Oliver Hickel and they live in Denver with their children Bryan and Kimberly.

DONALD S. GALBREATH

Donald S. Galbreath spent the first 12 years of his life on a ranch along East Birch Creek about five miles south of Pilot Rock, Oregon. His father and mother had homesteaded in the area, coming from Pennsylvania in 1915.

The first six years of elementary school were attended at Harmony School, a one-room country school, adjacent to his parent's ranch. He attended high school at LaGrande. After two years attending Eastern Oregon College and Oregon State College he entered the U. S. Army Air Corps in 1942. Eighteen months of overseas duty took him to East Greenland where his small outfit (20 men) built the only weather station ever built near the center of the Greenland Ice Cap where European weather is born.

Returning to civilian status he continued his education and obtained both a B.S. and an M.S. degree in Fish and Game Management. Don spent 32 years with the Washington State Department of Game as a regional game biologist. He did special research on both the chukar partridge and the ringnecked pheasant.

Upon retirement in 1979 he spent much time doing field research with his co-author, and nephew, Larry Nielsen on pioneer roads and pioneers in eastern Oregon.